ABANDONED TO JESUS

A CALL TO WHOLEHEARTED DISCIPLESHIP

KELLY SHAW

Abandoned to Jesus: A Call to Wholehearted Discipleship
By Kelly Shaw

Published by IGNITE Media

GMMI
100 County Rd. 263
Armstrong, MO 65230
www.globalmmi.net

First print 2023, Copyright 2023 by IGNITE Media
All Rights Reserved

ISBN (Print): 978-1-956435-23-8
ISBN (Digital): 978-1-956435-25-2

All Scripture quotations are taken from the New King James Version. Copyright 1982, Thomas Nelson,Inc.

Cover Design – Ruangrit Kanchai
Formatting Design - IGNITE Media

More copies of this writing can be ordered from www.globalmmi.com or by contacting info@globalmmi.com

Kelly Shaw can be personally contacted at kshaw@GlobalMMI.net.

"If there is any lesson that ongoing global crisis including the pandemic has taught us, it is that our ability to hold on when things look difficult depends on our centeredness in Christ and the extent to which one is being transformed into His image. In Abandoned to Jesus", Kelly Shaw provides a biblical framework that fosters "movements of the heart" for transformation and true discipleship. She also does a great job in unpacking four practices that can help believers in whatever stage of life to live an abandoned devotional lifestyle in Christ. It is a timely work that will be of great benefit to all who genuinely seek the grace of spiritual transformation and true discipleship." - *Fred Dimado, Associate International Director, PIONEERS*

"Kelly Shaw's book Abandoned to Jesus to new believers and mature believers alike. It is a challenge to develop a lifestyle of radical commitment with encouragement and insight into Scriptures that will lead to a continually deepening of one's relationship with the Lord Jesus. Abandoned to Jesus is about developing a lifestyle, knowing that God is not content to leave us where we are, but is continually calling us deeper from wherever we are." - *Dr. Elizabeth Glanville, Senior Assistant Professor of Leadership*

"If you desire a deeper walk with God and want to grow in your devotion to our Lord, then this is a must read. In this book Kelly Shaw challenges the reader to count Jesus more worthy of our affections than anything else in the world. She makes a clarion call for intimacy with God for Great Commission leaders, and highlights that we cannot lead people to have an experience with God that we ourselves have not experienced. She challenges leaders to prioritize the Great Commission in their discipleship journey with others and gives step by step priorities that are necessary to experience that intimate walk with Him. Kelly lives what she writes so this is not just a book but a lifestyle of hers, welcome to the abandoned devotion lifestyle." - *Tshepang Basupi, Executive Director, Southern Africa Region, Africa Inland Mission International*

"An outstanding book to read from a woman of God Kelly Shaw, who understands the essence and importance of Abandoned Devotion as essential in discipling the remaining unreached and unengaged people group of the world. It emphasizes the cost of discipleship by attaining spiritual deepness through the daily practice of Christian discipline, the willingness to sacrifice time, money, security, friends, and family in exchange of knowing Christ alone. It is very inspiring and instructive for anyone with a passion to disciple the church and the Nation." - *Pastor Jimmy Reyes Fundar, President, One Sending Body, The Mission Sending Arm of the Federation of Southern Baptist Convention in the Philippines*

"In an age of escalated anxiety, identity confusion and spiritual numbness that fosters sin and addiction, Kelly calls us to strengthen our foundations so we can live in intimate dependence on God. She writes in a relevant way to offer a biblical and practical roadmap that awakens a more vibrant faith and relationship with God and fosters spiritual abundance and protection. Because I've lived near Kelly, I've benefitted from and seen God do amazing things because she embodies what she has written in this book!" - *Ellen Peters, wife of Pioneers International Director Emeritus*

"In her recent book, Kelly Shaw provides Christian leaders with a helpful starting point for discipleship and growth. She outlines four movements and habits that undergird an active life of devotion to Jesus, encapsulated in the oxymoronic term, "abandoned devotion." The book continually challenges the reader to move beyond Bonhoeffer's "cheap grace," to a life of passion and immersion in scripture and prayer. This is done through the careful cultivation of inner disciplines which undergird a counter-cultural life as one called to provide leadership in the church. And, finally, throughout the book, Kelly continues to insist that the purpose of the Christian life has an evangelistic outcome in Jesus' passion and compassion for all people groups. Drawing on her own life and experience throughout the narrative, each chapter concludes with a set of helpful questions for application, as well as a prayer of blessing." - *Brian T. Hartley, Ph.D. |Professor and Dean Emeritus*

-

CONTENTS

Foreword

One of the most overlooked, yet fundamental aspects of mission mobilization is an emphasis on spiritual depth and wholehearted discipleship among believers across the global Church. It is difficult to mobilize our local ministries and churches to align with the redemptive purpose of God among all humanity if we first haven't settled the issue that Jesus is Lord, are surrendered to Christ, have given up all rights, desire His will more then our own and are living for His glory among all peoples on the earth. This is where mobilization begins and continues - calling disciples to live set apart for Him and His glory alone, while showing them how to become practically involved in various ways in the Great Commission.

I don't know of anyone better equipped to guide the way forward in this crucial subject matter then Kelly. Yes, she happens to be my wife (which means I am the luckiest man alive), but beyond that she is a student of what it means to faithfully live as a disciple of Jesus Christ. She has effectively taught this subject over the last 10 years of our GMMI Global Mobilization Institute training schools while faithfully living according to the precepts herself. Leaders in these programs love her teaching and are consistently cut to the heart with areas of conviction the Spirit points out through her insights and illustrations. Kelly is a stellar example of a leader following Jesus wholeheartedly, which means sacrificially and with an accompanying lifestyle of surrender.

If you are a mission, denomination, church network or organization leader you need to read this book and use it among your constituencies. Abandoned To Jesus provides the starting point to invite disciples in your spheres of influence to the joy and privilege of following Jesus as intended, with all our being. As you build on this fundamental foundation of abandonment to Jesus you will find believers increasingly desiring to walk in the will of God, laying down their lives sacrificially to do so among the unreached peoples, both near and distant. This book has the potential to launch a movement of wholehearted love for Jesus across the global body of Christ that culminates in prioritizing what He prioritizes.

I commend this important book, and all it stands for, to the reader. Don't just read it but commit to stop and pray through portions and aspects as the Spirit prompts you. Don't be in a hurry. Stop and dwell with the Lord as you meditate on the truths, principles and lifestyle revealed in this book.

Ryan Shaw
International Lead Facilitator
Global Mission Mobilization Initiative

Introduction

We are living in unprecedented times. A global pandemic has ravaged the globe, leaving a toll of human suffering from the highly contagious virus. However, the economic suffering from the lockdowns and the near collapse of the tourism industry globally has compounded the already fragile outlook by bankrupting many businesses and leaving many unemployed. The vast implications of the economic and global health crisis have brought many to complete desperation. In some parts of the world, the lack of medical supplies for the surging number of cases has left people dying in the streets unable to receive medical treatment. The inability and lack of resources to cope has caused some to just give up. Suicide rates have risen because of the desperation. The mental health professionals are seeing more adults and children with problems trying to navigate a post-Covid world. Many people have struggled with paralyzing fear; the fear of the unknown has become more real with a virus that is new to scientists and hard to predict.

The whole world is grappling with the new global realities. While the world wonders what is next, there remains a constant battle with the now and not yet. We keep thinking normal is right around the corner, but then a new wave breaks out. As the vaccines are rolled out, a new hope dawned. While this virus may soon come to an end, the economic impact will be felt for years to come. Normal is not right around the corner. Recovery is a process.

As this pandemic has brought to light the uncertainty of our globally interdependent world, we see the global realities shifting. The pandemic has ushered in a new transition in the way the world thinks and approaches life. The ability to make plans, travel, and do business has shifted. No longer are plans dependent upon one's self but upon the restrictions of various places.

Not only has the pandemic shifted our thinking about the way we do things, but it has also impacted the way we think about ourselves. In the midst of losing jobs and the struggle to survive, we are confronted with the reality of who we really are and how helpless we are without God. We cannot depend upon ourselves to get us out of the mess we are in, but we must look to the Lord Almighty as the Way, the Truth, and the Light through this darkness. Here in the uncertainty, the Church must arise as a beacon of light and hope to a world sinking in the darkness and mire. But it is impossible for the Church to be that light without the followers of Jesus living holy lives, completely abandoned to Jesus.

For many believers, the pandemic has brought to light deeper issues. Often, our identity has revolved around the things we do. Our job where we have been so successful in the past is suddenly gone. Now, we have to struggle with our identity without that job. The loss of economic stability has brought to light our dependence upon a job as our provider rather than looking to the Lord as Source. The loss of certainty has caused depression, and we need to look to the "Rock" that is higher than us for that stability in our lives. All of these issues existed before the pandemic, but the crisis has caused them to become more pronounced. This crisis will fade, but these issues must be dealt with in order to grow in our relationship with God.

The list of things we could not do over the last year has grown exponentially, whether schooling, meetings, travel, business, and much more. Basing our identity around doing things, we have felt restless and unsuccessful doing nothing. For Christians, even the mere routine of going to church has been disrupted. We have gone through lockdowns; we have lived life online, Zoom meetings for work, Zoom meetings for church, and Zoom meetings for school. Our busy worlds of sports and activities came to a standstill. Leaving behind the busyness, we have been challenged by the stillness to consider something deeper.

In the stillness, we consider the root of what it means to be successful, what it means to not be full of anxiety, what it means to not be lonely. The root of these causes is found in relationship with Jesus. For many, the measuring stick of success is how we are doing in our profession. In ministry, our success becomes based on the responses of other people, how well our ministry is known, how influential we are in our ministry, the number of people attending our meetings. But these statistics only describe the type of work we do.

Rather, we need to see our work does not define us. When work is our identity and we lose our job, we easily fall into a tailspin of depression because our identity is gone. In ministry, we might be on the field, faithfully sharing the gospel and praying for revival but we do not see anyone turning to Christ. Are we a failure because of a lack of numbers to report to our sending church? Are we a failure because our ministry isn't the biggest or most influential?

While we all can affirm that God has called us to do certain things for His Kingdom, we must be careful to not let the measure of those things become the measure of our lives before God. Rather than basing our lives in the doing, we need to change the standard to one that is foundational: Who are we becoming? Rather than being defined by our work, our identity must be rooted in the character and quality of our inner life with God.

We are not all of the activities we do; we are not the job we do every day; we are not just the title of a relationship to others – mother, father, sister, brother, wife, husband, or child. We are a child of God. We are

His beloved and He is our Beloved. We need a vibrant relationship with our Father in heaven where we can thrive in adversity because it causes us to draw closer to Him. We need a faith seeking to embrace the challenges as opportunities to see God move in power. Refusing to allow fear to paralyze us, we are called to confident hope in God's ways and love for us.

King David rooted his identity wholly in God. Long after the history books of David's life had been written and all of his sin recorded in detail in the pages of Scripture, Paul proclaims God's testimony about David's life, "And when He (God) had removed him (Saul), He (God) raised up for them David as King, to whom also He gave testimony and said, 'I have found David the son of Jesse, a man after My own heart, who will do all My will'" (Acts 13:22). The testimony of David's life was not all the great things that he accomplished, neither all the wars that he won nor reuniting the tribes of Israel under his leadership, nor was his testimony all of the sin he committed throughout his life. His testimony was who he became, "a man after God's own heart." The heart of true discipleship is tested in who we are becoming. Our identity is refined through the adversity we face and solidified in our joyful surrender to Him over and over again.

In the Christian life, there is only one standard of success, Jesus Christ, against whom everyone stands on a fair playing field. In Him, we all have equal access. We are all equally forgiven of our sins. We have all had pasts with a few too many ugly marks on the sketch board of history. Yet, for every one of our sins and mistakes, Christ's blood wipes it whiter than snow for a new history to be drawn in those places. Background and education, ethnicity and wealth are all non-existent factors when it comes to relationship with Almighty God. He cares not which school we attended, what neighborhood we grew up in, what color our skin is, or how much money our family has. The standard for each one remains the same: deeply knowing and walking with the Lord.

So, we must ask ourselves, "If being image bearers of Christ is the standard of success, how then shall we live?" Jesus definitely cares about the smallest details of our lives, but His ultimate concern is a picture much bigger than that. If we think of it like a painting, each stroke of the brush contributes to the painting as a whole. Without small brush strokes, we would never end up with a painting but only an empty canvas. So, if each brush stroke is representative of the decisions we make every day, those decisions are shaping the image that we are becoming. The Lord is desiring for the image we are becoming to be reflective of the image of Christ and aligning with His plans and purposes. As we bear His image, we then make choices that reflect His heart. In the same way, the choices that we make each day are conforming us to His image.

One key of being conformed to the image of Christ that is not often emphasized in the Church today is God's passion for all the peoples of the earth. Earlier we talked about King David being a "man after God's own heart." David was the king of Israel, but he was supremely aware of God's heartbeat for all nations, not just Israel. As we read the Psalms, we are reminded over and again of God's desire for His praise to resound from every people group on earth. Similarly, as we choose to be conformed to the image of Christ, our hearts will reflect the heart of the Father. God's heart is to have all peoples, tribes and languages worshipping before His throne (Revelation 7:9). True disciples will echo the heart of the Father, being passionately consumed with a desire to see His name glorified in all the earth.

Sadly, the way we have often heard the message of us being conformed to Christ's image tends to be a reactionary rather than an intentional approach. Jesus didn't only respond to the situations that confronted Him, but rather He cultivated a life reflective of the Father. We cannot expect to know the will of God if we are not cultivating a life of going deep with Jesus and, out of relationship, knowing what we should do in each circumstance.

As leaders in ministry, we get caught in the busyness of moving from one activity to the other and in the need to have something to report in our newsletter. Instead, we want to move away from the need to be busy and to instead be prayerfully aligned with what we see the Father doing. Making purposeful choices to engage and depend upon the Lord for our fruitfulness in ministry as well as changing the measuring stick of our success from outward numbers to inward intimacy. These movements will change our overall thrust of ministry.

The average Christian says they have a quiet time, which often means only 5-10 minutes of reading something in the Bible. But this reality of relationship goes beyond simply having a quiet time every day. While this is a beautiful start to a deeper relationship with God, the intimacy of knowing Him comes as we truly deny ourselves and choose to live in the Spirit. Life in the Spirit comes from the deep abiding in Christ, day in and day out, choosing to focus our hearts and our minds on things above, taking every thought captive, and being proactive rather than just reacting to circumstances.

In this book, I will examine the Christian life in terms of our goal of being conformed to the image of Christ and propose proactive steps to get there as well as habits that will keep us continually walking in this way and the resulting heartbeat for the nations. In graduate school, I took an independent study class on the writings of Henri Nouwen. As I read thousands of pages of his writings, I was overwhelmed with a verse in Galatians. Paul writes,

> *I have been crucified with Christ, and I no longer live, but Christ lives in me. The life I live in the flesh, I live by faith in the Son of God who loved me and gave Himself up for me (2:20).*

The Christian life is not about me living MY life for Christ, but instead it is me allowing Christ to live HIS life in me. We have been bought with a price, Christ's death on the cross. As a child of the Father, His highest aspiration for us is to be more like His Son.

We are all called to be His witnesses: sharing what we have received, teaching what we have learned, and impacting the world around us with the fragrance of Christ inside of us. This is the essence of the gospel as not for me only but to be shared with others. However, we can only do this as we are being transformed on the inside so the fragrance inside is stronger than the fragrance of the world.

Let us first examine this call of being abandoned to Jesus as beginning with our being conformed to the image of Christ and then understand some key qualities His children are called to possess. Our goal in becoming like Christ is not meant only for ourselves. As we are internalizing these truths, we are also called to teach them to others (Matthew 5:19). This is how we will disciple the nations and be the blessing that Abraham was promised (Matthew 28:18-20; Genesis 12:1-3).

1

What Is Abandoned Devotion?

Many Christians today believe they are living the fullness of life with God. But they have only touched the surface of that fullness because they have never been shown the way to go deeper. Those who walk on the surface level enjoy going to church on Sundays, reading the Bible, and praying, but their experience of God is not shaping who they are, and neither is it being a transforming influence on those around them. God's desire is for our faith to go much deeper and for it to be a transforming power in the world.

The nature of true faith is its transforming power. Paul writes in 2 Corinthians 3:18, "But we all... are being transformed into the same image from glory to glory." It is vital to appreciate that this process of transformation is not a passive process. It is not merely a question of showing up. Jesus is not interested in believers who go to church in order to check a box on a list. Jesus wants us to become true disciples who are passionately pursuing God and being transformed into His likeness in the process.

In talking to people from across the global body of Christ, we find a lack of depth permeating the church. In many cultures, a gospel of prosperity is invading the church where there is no substantive discussion of the place of suffering in living for Christ. In other places, we find a gospel of faith that is devoid of works. They say, "Believing is enough; I don't need to do anything about it." Their faith for prosperity is consistent, but they are not allowing their faith to transform the way they treat others, to transform their pride, or to embrace the calling to die to self. These doctrines have been based on one part of the gospel, which is true, but it is elevated to the near absence of other prominent themes in the Bible. Imagine a body where one leg is five times the size of the other leg and the rest of the body. The person could do nothing because everything is out of proportion. This lack of balance in the body of Christ has made us dysfunctional and unable to see God's Kingdom purposes and plans fulfilled in His Church.

God is calling for a new depth of discipleship firmly rooted and grounded in the gospel. We cannot hope to move others toward living relationship without helping them to understand the fullness of God's Word and commands. In fact, the Great Commission from Jesus is our roadmap for true discipleship. He states, "Go and make disciples" (Matthew 28:19-20). We have to go to the darkness and begin sharing the gospel of the Kingdom, God's ways, God's character, God's purposes – and as we share, we are making disciples. Once they have decided to make a public commitment, then they are baptized and we begin teaching the habits of what it means to walk fully committed to Jesus. We don't have to wait for discipleship until after they are baptized. We disciple people before they even make that decision. However, after they make the commitment, we cannot leave them there. We need to teach them how to live in the Kingdom. This is the step that is often left out. We help people enter the door to the Kingdom and think we are done, but we are only at the beginning of the process of becoming His Bride.

Here, Jesus gives the insight into this depth we have been looking for all along. Through the baptism into Christ's Kingdom, we are brought in through repentance and, as John said of Jesus' baptism, *"with the Holy Spirit and fire"* (Matthew 3:11). This same necessity of repentance and the need for the Holy Spirit is repeated in the Great Commission passages in Mark, Luke, John and Acts. We cannot expect to live in the fullness of God without repentance and the Holy Spirit. The other key Jesus highlights is the many truths He has already taught them. We will begin to unfold the depths of what Jesus taught as the keys to the life of true discipleship in His Kingdom.

This depth of true discipleship is what is embodied in the *abandoned devotion lifestyle*. Discipleship is not something we do. Discipleship is about who we are becoming. Unfortunately for us, we cannot become true disciples in one day. This is why we talk about not just abandoned devotion but the *abandoned devotion lifestyle*. We are called to walk out our discipleship day after day, but not in a monotonous rigor of always doing the same things. Rather, we are called to grow up and mature in Christ so that today we are learning new things about God that we did not know yesterday. This is how we truly come into the fullness of life with God.

Understanding the Term 'Abandoned Devotion'

The word "abandoned" has a strong meaning and often strong emotion attached to it. Most often, it is construed as something negative. The word conjures up pictures of children who have been abandoned, left utterly alone, needing to depend completely upon themselves, unable to trust anyone else. In many cultures, there is also the reality of fathers leaving their wives and children to fend for themselves. They have been abandoned. The definition describes one who is abandoned as forsaken. One who is abandoned is forgotten by the ones who are supposed to care most deeply.

Applying this word "abandoned" to devotion, some people might think it means to abandon one's devotion or faith in Jesus. Some have even considered it to be forsaking Jesus completely. The confusion comes from the juxtaposition of two words with such strong meaning – "abandoned" meaning forsaking, next to "devotion," meaning profound dedication or consecration. Normally, these two words in combination would suggest forsaking dedication and consecration.

However, it means completely the opposite. Abandoned devotion is to forsake all else in pursuit of Jesus alone. "Abandoned" serves to describe the totality and extent of our devotion. Our devotion is no longer casual, comfortable or convenient. This abandoned devotion calls us to live that way when it costs us our time, money, security, friends and family. We need to grasp the depths of our dependence upon the Lord and Him alone. John wrote in his gospel of Jesus, *"Without me, you can do nothing"* (John 15:5). This is the depth of dependence we must pursue. We do not respond only when it is convenient, but we surrender everything to Jesus.

Why Live the Abandoned Devotion Lifestyle?

Abandoned devotion is key for believers because we cannot give to someone else something that we do not possess ourselves. God's call on our lives as believers is to be disciples who are making other disciples, but we cannot teach someone something that we have not yet learned. This holds true for pastors, message bearers, and other ministry leaders. We cannot expect our congregations to be full of fire and passion for Jesus if we do not first hold this passion ourselves. We cannot expect others to grasp the fullness of what it means to forsake all else if we have not first committed ourselves to forsaking all else in pursuit of one thing, Jesus Christ.

James Robert Clinton refers to this idea as what we do flowing out of who we are. He explains this saying that God created us not as human "doings" but human "beings." In other words, who we are is not what we do but who we are informs, characterizes, and energizes the ministry we do.[1] His particular audience was ministry leaders as he taught at Fuller Theological Seminary for many years. I would take this a step further to say that, as followers of Jesus, the life we live on the outside is in direct correlation to the life we are cultivating on the inside. We need to get away from the idea of becoming a Christian and then just coasting along until we reach heaven. Our time here on Earth is our training ground in becoming true branches bearing the power and fruitfulness of the Vine to whom we are connected.

One of my students told me that in her country pastors are highly respected, much as doctors are in the West. She explained that many people want to become pastors because it is a great job to have. These pastors are interested in helping their congregations, but once they receive a position as pastor, they no longer grow in their understanding of God. Their identity becomes rooted in the position they hold instead of rooted in knowing God more and being His child. Therefore, they begin what some call plateauing, where one reaches a certain height of knowledge or experience and stops growing and pursuing new experiences. But, as we go deeper in God, we realize that if we are not pressing into God then we are really slipping away. The little foxes of sin, such as not wanting to read the Word and compromising in seemingly small areas or being lazy to not do the things we know we should, start to creep in and steal our joy in Jesus and in following Him. We begin to make other things more important than spending time in God's presence. These may seem small at first, but it is these small steps, going uncorrected, that become a slippery slope into deep deception and sin.

To avoid the little foxes and the slippery slope, abandoned devotion must become a continual lifestyle. Sometimes in our excitement after we receive Jesus into our hearts, we start off well, forsaking those things hindering our love for Jesus. But as the days wear on, we simply get tired of saying no, and we slip back into old patterns and habits. It is easy to get caught up in the busyness of life, to become distracted by the pursuit of a better job or helping our family. Anything we fail to put in line with God's priorities can quickly become a stumbling block to abandoned devotion in our lives.

Jesus is pursuing a growing wholeheartedness in our lives. He desires for us to get rid of more of our sin nature today than we did yesterday. He wants us to experience more victory over temptation today than we did yesterday. This process unfolds in the daily choices we make to keep saying "yes" to the still small voice leading us toward our greatest desire, our Beloved. Day after day, week after week, month after month, year after year, we choose to surrender; we choose to go deeper; we choose to say no to distractions; we choose to forsake all over and over again in pursuit of knowing God more and loving Him with our whole heart.

Why Is Abandoned Devotion Necessary?

A common response to this theme of abandoned devotion is: "I have been living my Christian life just fine until now, why should I change?" Change is hard. Change takes work. Why can't the disciplines of attending church, going to Bible study, and having a regular quiet time be enough? If we are merely doing works on the outside and our heart is not being changed in the process, then we are missing the mark.

I do not personally like to miss the mark. One of the things that is both my greatest strength and weakness is my tendency toward perfectionism. Perfectionism is good because it causes me to strive for excellence, doing everything with 100% of my effort, not giving into compromise or cutting corners. However, it is also the thing that brings me the most condemnation because I will never be perfect, and I continually miss the mark. In order to avoid missing the mark, I like to know exactly what is expected of me. In school, when I would have to write a paper or take a test, I would find out exactly what was supposed to be written and the material needed for the test so I could achieve the best result.

In the Christian life, if we don't want to miss the mark in our relationship with God, we need to know what is expected. What is Christ looking for? In the gospels, we hear the phrase, *"Well done, good and faithful servant."* If we want to hear that phrase, what are the requirements we need to meet? If we want to know what Jesus is expecting so we are not surprised, then we must begin by understanding some of what is written in the Bible about what He is expecting to find at His return.

In Matthew 25, we read the parable of the ten virgins waiting for the return of the bridegroom. This well-known parable tells of how five wise virgins took their lamps filled with oil and brought extra oil to wait for the bridegroom. At the same time, five foolish virgins took their lamps with no extra oil and waited for the bridegroom as well. They all fell asleep waiting for the bridegroom, but when the cry came that the bridegroom had returned, the wise ran to the bridegroom but the foolish were delayed because they had no oil left, only lamps. While the foolish virgins went to buy oil, the bridegroom came; those who were ready entered in and the door was shut. The foolish came later, crying, *"Lord, Lord, open to us!"* But Jesus replied, *"Assuredly, I say to you, I do not know you."*

This parable lays out both the good news and the bad news. I would suggest that the lamp represents our decision to follow Christ and the oil represents the Holy Spirit. All ten virgins had lamps with a little oil. They had all made decisions to follow Christ at some point, and at the same time had received a measure of the Holy Spirit. The five wise virgins brought with them extra oil. This extra oil represents the living relationship they have cultivated over the years: time spent reading the Scriptures; time spent praying; time spent quiet before the throne listening to the Spirit; time repeatedly spent obeying what they heard before the throne.

These actions of the wise virgins in this parable demonstrate why they are called "wise." The foolish ask them for some of their oil, but the wise tell them they must go and buy oil for themselves. True intimacy is not something we can get from someone else's life with God. A believer cannot grow in their relationship with the Lord by only depending upon hearing a sermon on Sunday or hearing testimonies of what God is doing in the lives of others. Hearing these things might challenge a believer, but unless they choose to apply this knowledge or do something different, nothing will change. We must experience the life-changing power of the gospel in our own lives. We must listen to the Spirit and respond ourselves. For those who have believed and continue to have a living, vibrant relationship with the Lord, filled with the intimacy of walking closely with God and being filled with His Spirit, they will be ushered into the great banquet feast with the bridegroom.

However, five of the virgins could represent those who do not continue to walk in close relationship with Jesus, just reading His Word and praying. They do not receive a continual filling of the Holy Spirit. They do not continue to be refreshed by the fountain of living water. They came to faith but never take any steps to grow in their faith. Thus, they have not developed their relationship with God and have no intimacy; and Jesus will say to them, *"I do not know you."* This statement by Jesus, "I do not know you," is a powerful testimony of what Christ is expecting. He wants to know us and in the same manner for us to know Him. This parable also suggests that intimacy requires more of us than a decision. It requires a lifestyle.

Before we were married, my husband and I were dating, but we lived thousands of miles apart. We had to be very purposeful in our communication in order to grow in our relationship. We would write long letters to each other during the week via email, and on the weekends, we would talk on the phone. This process of intentional and deep conversation developed an intimacy and strength, laying the foundation of our relationship that has continued to grow over the years we have been married. If we had not been purposeful in our communication, then the relationship would have died for lack of time spent cultivating our relationship. In the same way, we are called to be intentional in developing our relationship with the Lord.

But sadly, when I go to coffee shops these days, I see people who are on dates, and supposedly trying to get to know one another, but all they are really doing is looking at their phones. Just because two people occupy the same space does not mean they are getting to know one another. In the same way, we can do the same thing in our spiritual lives. People go to church or Bible study and are around others who have passionate hearts for God, but nothing in their lives changes as a result of that experience. We might read the Bible, but if it is only increasing our knowledge without impacting our behavior, it is useless.

Pictures of Abandoned Devotion

To understand what abandoned devotion looks like, it is helpful to begin with a familiar picture demonstrating what it means to be willing to forsake all in pursuit of Jesus alone. Let us first take the story of the four fishermen Jesus called to be His disciples.

> *And as He walked by the Sea of Galilee, He saw Simon and Andrew his brother casting a net into the sea; for they were fishermen. Then Jesus said to them, 'Follow Me, and I will make you become fishers of men.' They immediately left their nets and followed Him. When He had gone a little farther from there, He saw James the son of Zebedee, and John his brother, who also were in the boat mending their nets. And immediately He called them, and they left their father Zebedee in the boat with the hired servants, and went after Him* (Mark 1:16-20).

This brief account of Jesus calling His disciples has great significance for us as we consider this term abandoned devotion. Peter, Andrew, James and John were willing to leave behind all that was familiar, all that was comfortable, all that was known, all that was dear, including their own father, to go after a Man. This is a picture of abandoned devotion. It is a willingness to count Jesus as more worthy of our affections than anything else this world can offer, which is our first and most important step toward true discipleship.

We must ask ourselves why these men would willingly leave all to follow this Man Jesus. Jesus was a carpenter by trade, not a fisherman. He was likely a gifted carpenter and well respected in his profession. He walks up to these men who are experienced fishermen and calls them to "follow" Him, and He will make them "fishers of men."

Luke expands on the details of this calling. He emphasizes that Simon was there in the boat with Jesus, having just listened to Jesus teach the multitudes. Then Jesus asks Simon to launch out into the deep after he just spent the whole night fishing and caught nothing. Simon, exhausted and seeing no logic in what Jesus was asking, was moved to obedience because of the authority and power with which Jesus had taught the multitudes. Simon's obedience leads to a miraculous catch of more fish than one boat or net could bear. After hearing Jesus' teaching and seeing the miracle, Simon, Andrew, James and John were moved to wholeheartedly say "yes" to follow Jesus and leave everything behind. The wondrous amount of spiritual authority on those words gripped their very hearts.

Jesus offers this path of discipleship to several people throughout the gospels. Mostly, we think of the disciples themselves. But one of the others He speaks to about discipleship is the rich young ruler who is honestly, earnestly seeking a deeper life and the rich reward of eternal life.

The rich young ruler pursued Jesus, running after Him, unwilling to let this opportunity pass to gain a deeper level of truth. The young man knelt before Jesus in respect to the authority and power he had seen this Man display. Then he called Jesus, "Good Teacher," which Jesus reminded him is a term reserved for God alone, hinting at the truth that this young man had grasped.

In answer to the young man's question of what one must do to inherit eternal life, Jesus reminded him of the commandments. But the young man was quick to point out that he had kept these since he was very young. However, Jesus explained that, though he thought he had kept the commandments, he had not understood the full implications of these commandments. He thought he had not worshipped any idol, but his wealth had become the one thing that was holding him back from embracing the fullness of true discipleship.

Unfortunately, when the young man was confronted with truth, he could not embrace it. He was unwilling to give that which would cost him something. The life of true discipleship calls us beyond our own strength and abilities and to depend wholly upon Jesus as our source. Jesus was not asking the young man to sell all he had in order to make him suffer. Jesus was asking him where he placed the most value – on things that he could see or on those things not seen?

From this, we understand this term abandoned devotion more fully. Abandoned devotion is not just following a set of rules. The young man had tried that route and, while succeeding in his own mind, had, in truth, failed miserably because of a lack of spiritual understanding. Rules without spiritual understanding lead us to become like the Pharisees. If we do what the pastor says only because he says we should or should not do it, then we are merely following the rules without understanding the heart of the matter.

Jesus is first calling us to life that yearns for the deeper substance of truth. Throughout Scripture, we hear an oft-repeated phrase of having eyes but not seeing, ears but not hearing, and a heart but with no understanding. (Deut. 29:4; Is. 6:9, 42:20; Jer. 5:21; Ezek.12:2; Matt. 13:14; Mk 8:18; John 12:40; Rom. 11:8) One of the places we see this is in Jesus' parables. We need to be those who desire the meat of God's Word, living understanding, and a hunger to comprehend the deep mysteries of God's Kingdom (Heb. 5:12-14). Our hungering after God should lead us to constantly study God's Word to know Him more, understand more of His ways, and gain a deeper revelation of His character.

Abandoned devotion also involves a cost. The rich young ruler was unwilling to pay this cost. The price was too high. Rather, a heart of true devotion will respond as King David did: *"I will not give to God that which costs me nothing"* (2 Sam. 24:24). In giving to God, we find joy and freedom in our hearts. To the world, denying ourselves seems harsh and counterintuitive. Wouldn't we want things that are good and right? But as we set our hearts to follow the Lord, we see our hearts are deceitfully wicked and often lead us astray. The path to freedom is not fulfilling the desires of the flesh but denying ourselves in order to follow Jesus.

In order to be willing to deny ourselves, we must redefine what true treasure is in life. Is treasure what will get us ahead in life? Is treasure what will make us rich? What is treasure or truly precious in our eyes? Treasure, according to Jesus, will make us rich, but not materially or financially. It will not put us ahead in the world's eyes or according to worldly standards. True treasure is being conformed to Christ's image. This is God's highest priority in our lives.

When our treasure is to become like Christ, we will gladly pay any price to see it come to pass. Paul wrote, *"But we have this treasure in earthen vessels, that the excellence of the power may be of God and not of us"* (2 Cor. 4:7). Paul understood that this treasure God is calling us to bear within us is the very life and image of His Son. Our power comes from God's life and image at work within us. As we are daily conformed more and more into His image, God releases more power through our lives.

Here we come to the heart of the issue. Today in the body of Christ, there is a tendency to live according to the superficial understanding of the commandments like the rich young ruler. People do only what they think is absolutely necessary. They go to church and read the Bible, but those activities flow out of hearts that merely want to do their duty. The goal of the Christian life is not to just be saved: God's highest calling on our lives is to be made in the image and likeness of Christ.

This is true discipleship. Abandoned devotion requires a cost, a cost many are unwilling to pay because their priorities and treasure do not align with Christ's calling on their lives. Christ does not call only part of a person. He calls us to give our whole selves unto Him. Abandoned devotion is an invitation to a deeper level of intimacy, understanding and power. Abandoned devotion is a commitment to embrace the cost, to endure and persevere over a lifetime, and to finish well. Abandoned devotion is to wholeheartedly give oneself to becoming like Christ in every way. The abandoned devotion lifestyle is not easy, but the rewards are great.

The *abandoned devotion lifestyle* can be broken down into four movements that take us deeper in relationship with God and, repeated over and over again throughout the course of one's life, will enable us to finish well. The entry point into *the abandoned devotion lifestyle* is brokenness. From here, we develop wholeheartedness, which leads to deeper understanding of God's character and ways. This revelation causes us to want to respond in complete obedience. The four activities that undergird the movement from brokenness to obedience are devotion to studying the Bible, spending time in prayer, fasting regularly, and engaging in spiritual warfare. Consistently engaging in these activities will enable us to continue cultivating the four movements in our lives.

Abandoned Devotion and the Great Commission

As we delve into growing in abandoned devotion, it is important to remember the goal of God's transforming work in our lives is not for us alone. From the beginning of the Bible until the end, we see the heartbeat of God for us to live in community. But being more than just a passive member of the community is expected of us. Once we have received the truth, God expects us to teach others to do the same (Matt. 5:19). It is this natural outward thrust of the Kingdom that all true believers possess. We will see this as we go through the next several chapters and look at God's calling to transform the world around us through the power of the Spirit as we are in relationship with others. Every believer is supposed to be this transforming light in whatever sphere of influence the Lord has placed us, whether at work, on a baseball team, at a university, in our neighborhood, etc.

The call to proclaim the gospel of the Kingdom is a natural by-product of a lifestyle of abandoned devotion. We are not only a transforming influence, but we are engaged in mobilizing others toward the Great Commission. Whether through prayer, giving, going, advocating, mobilizing or welcoming, we can all be engaged in the Great Commission. *The abandoned devotion lifestyle* calls us to prioritize the

Great Commission in our discipleship of others and in our daily lives. Abandoned devotion fuels our alignment with God and His purposes in the Earth.

Not only is abandoned devotion connected to our living in community, but it challenges our notion of what is necessary for those going out as message bearers in the Great Commission. Message bearers who are like the five foolish virgins who have merely accepted Christ but do not have a vibrant, active relationship with the Lord will easily be overcome by the pressures on the field. The deepening of the spiritual life is the key to thrusting the Church into the harvest. A Church that is on fire will be drawn into God's heart for the nations. Andrew Murray analyzed the connection between the spiritual life and missionaries sent out. He stated,

> The principal lesson the C.M.S. [Church Missionary Society] history teaches is that its great forward movement was intimately connected with a deep revival of spiritual life, and the teaching of a higher standard of devotion to the Lord Jesus. The only way to waken true, deep, spiritual, permanent missionary interest, is not to aim at this itself, so much as to lead believers to a more complete separation from the world, and to an entire consecration of themselves, with all they have to their Lord and His service.[2]

Whether through giving into the temptation of sin, ineffectiveness, or any of the many pitfalls the enemy would use to take them out, they will be easily overcome. Abandoned devotion enables believers to be those who, through much testing and trials, press through and persevere to see God's Kingdom established in all the earth.

Another challenge is for those message bearers who go to the field but allow the pressing demands of ministry to crowd out the necessary time that must be spent with God. Before they know it, it has been a month since they have had time to open their Bible and have a meaningful quiet time, much less, time to seek God's face in extended prayer. This lack of continually cultivating a deep relationship with the Lord will eventually lead to burnout. They have allowed urgent requests to rob time from the principal work. The Lord will not make us spend time with Him. However, the inevitable effect of not being connected to the Vine is that the branches wither and die. When we cease to be connected to the Lord, we succumb to the pressures of ministry and the world that are external to us. Yet, the Lord desires for us to look to Him to find the measure of what we need to do.

Finally, as we look at the Great Commission, not only are we all called to be witnesses, not only are we called to send out laborers, but these laborers are called to make disciples and teach them. The difficulty with message bearers who are not growing in abandoned devotion is that the quality of disciples they are making on the field will be of the same quality or less than they are. We cannot lead someone deeper in the Lord than we have gone ourselves. We cannot lead people in experiencing more of God than we have experienced ourselves. Teaching them from the Bible with the experiential understanding of God in those concepts will lack the spiritual authority necessary for these truths to produce fruit in their lives. The test of our relationship with God is to look at the fruit. The only way to produce lasting, eternal fruit that is transforming in its very nature is to be connected to the Vine, living abandoned devotion as a lifestyle.

Contemplation:

As we begin our journey toward *the abandoned devotion lifestyle*, we must first consider where we are personally in this journey. If we only think of this in terms of someone else, we will make no progress ourselves. Are you living the everyday Christian life according to rules and regulations? When you are tempted, do you say – "Jesus said I should not do that" or do you respond – "I don't want to do that because I know it will separate me from Jesus"? Do you just do what you have to do to be called a Christian? Or do you long to kneel before Jesus in prayer out of desire for relationship with Him? True relationship is filled with longing, desire, and conversation, and most of all it is enjoyable.

We don't want to condemn anyone. Rather, we want to stir a desire and willingness to go after more of God than we have today. All Christians should say with a resounding, "YES!" that they want more of Jesus today than they did yesterday. Our desire to become like Christ should be stronger and our commitment to surrender should be deeper with every passing moment. No one is exempt because no one is perfect… not until that day we stand face to face with the Perfectly Holy One.

1. In reflecting on the two pictures of abandoned devotion from the gospels, do we find ourselves more like the disciples who are willing to leave it all? Or are we like the rich young ruler who when asked to forsake it all could not leave his wealth? Take a moment to ask the Lord if there is something holding you back from wholehearted devotion. It is not necessarily money. It could be a relationship with someone. It could be a job you are doing to please yourself or someone else, but it isn't in alignment with the Lord's desire for you.

2. In reflecting on the idea of "doing" versus "being," have you unwittingly subscribed to the idea you are what you do? If I just do this, then everyone will be happy. True believers cannot live their lives to please themselves or others. We must relinquish the pressures of measuring up to lay hold of the unconditional love of the Father. We must choose to find our identity as His sons and daughters who have been purchased by the blood of His Son, Jesus Christ. We cannot hold onto pleasing others and at the same time understand the fullness of the love of God. As long as we find fulfillment in doing, we will never be truly satisfied to "be" His children. We are His delight, His joy, and that is enough.

Prayer:

Holy Spirit, I have tasted of something more. I want to find my identity completely in You. I want to be confident in belonging to You, having the depth of relationship of knowing how much You love me. My love for You is weak. I want to want more of You. Make me hungry for your presence. Make me thirsty for more of You, Holy Spirit. Increase my desire for the deeper life and greater intimacy with You. Here I am a Christian and yet I feel so empty. Help me to understand how to live my life fully connected to the Vine. In Jesus' name I pray, AMEN.

PART I:
Movements of the Abandoned Devotion Lifestyle

2

Brokenness
An Invitation to the Deeper Life

We begin our journey with the end in mind. God's highest calling and greatest hope for each one of His beloved children is to be made and formed in the image of Christ. His Son is the perfect One who not only died for us to have life, but He lived a sinless life as the image of God in the flesh for us to follow. We are not called to be people who can say, "Yes, I don't want to go to hell." We are called to be people who say, "Yes, I want to follow that Man Jesus because I have never known another like Him." How do we move from eternal assurance to a new reality now?

Often when we think of coming to salvation, we think of the joy we receive through the forgiveness of our sins. King David writes in the Psalms, *"Restore to me the joy of Your salvation, and uphold me by Your generous Spirit"* (Ps. 51:12). This joy comes from the cleansing of Christ's blood washing us of the sins we have committed. Being clean on the inside produces freedom and joy because we have been set free from guilt and shame.

Repentance

No longer do we bear the stain of sin. The prophet Isaiah described the stain of our sin, "'*Come now, and let us reason together,*' *says the Lord. 'Though your sins are like scarlet, they shall be as white as snow; though they are red like crimson, they shall be as wool*'" (Isaiah 1:18). Our sin is deep red, and no soap on Earth will wash it away. But the blood of Jesus applied to our stain of sin will wash it as white as snow. It seems kind of ironic that applying blood to a red stain would wash it white again. Yet, this is the gospel. Only the sinless blood of Christ can take away our sin. God does not have to work on our stain by scrubbing it and applying stain remover or bleach. Neither can we work to get the stain out. There is only one solution that instantly dissolves away the stain: Christ's blood. This remedy works on any stain of sin no matter how large or small, no matter what kind; it is all sin, and it is all covered by Christ's blood.

As the stain of our sin is washed away, we are overjoyed because our shame is gone. A weight has been lifted, and we are free. So why are we talking about brokenness being the entry point into the deeper life with God if every believer comes to repentance when they become a believer? What is the difference between salvation and this deeper life? Because as we journey on from the time of our salvation, we begin to realize we still sin. We still do things we know we should not do.

We must remember in the Christian life that we are serving the victorious, risen Lord. He has all power that is unstoppable. Christ's victory on the cross defeated every power of sin, every scheme of the enemy, even taking out the enemy's final victory in death. Christ is now seated at the right hand of the Father, interceding for us to live the life He intended for us. He has overcome everything. He wants us to live in that same victorious power. Yet, it seems we live at a level of less than what is promised. Most Christians are not living victorious lives. They go to church and do the right things, but their inner lives are characterized by turmoil and bondage; they are unable to break free of certain habits and sin.

There is a great conflict within us between always wanting to follow the Scriptures, and ending up doing what is often opposite of what God's Word says. Paul described his experience, *"For the good that I will to do, I do not do; but the evil I will not to do, that I practice"* (Romans 7:19). This is a very common experience for every believer. We want to do the right thing, but inevitably we end up doing the wrong thing.

I myself have had this same experience. I had accepted Christ in a small church where my sister had taken me, but it was not my home church. Not long after, my sister went to college and could no longer take me to that church. So, there I was with an experience of salvation but having no idea what to do next. During the next few years, I tried hard to do those things I thought would help me become a better Christian. I memorized Scriptures with my mom, and I read the Bible every day. But I found myself still doing things I knew were not what God wanted for me.

When I turned 16, I passed my driver's license test, and I was thrilled about this new step toward maturity and independence. A few months after getting my license, a friend and I were going to meet on a Saturday to go shopping together. On my way to meet her, I was driving on a narrow, curvy, country road paved with blacktop but with rock on the shoulders. Nearing a sharp curve, I slowed down and a car coming from the other direction drifted into the middle of the road and over the yellow line. Afraid the car might continue toward me, I pulled off the road slightly to give the car more room, slowing even more as the tires spun in the rock.

With a sigh of relief that danger had been averted, the car passed without hitting me. I gently nudged my car back into the right lane but the car drifted into the left lane. Thinking I had just overcorrected out of anxiety, I calmly and carefully nudged the car to the right lane once again. However, this time something totally unexpected happened. The car sharply turned 90 degrees to the right, and I looked up to see a giant 14-foot embankment of dirt rise immediately before me. I saw my brief life flash in pictures before my eyes, realizing there was nothing

I could do. Then, just as the front license plate hit the embankment, the car quickly turned again another 90 degrees. Now, riding in the ditch, I was going back the direction I had come from. Before I could react, the car turned yet again, except this time it did a 180 spin move where the back left corner of the car hit the embankment, sending the car over onto its side. After skidding 50 feet in the middle of the road with the car on its side, I finally came to a stop.

Another huge sigh of relief. I had sustained no major injuries, but I quickly realized I was still in danger. The road I was on was very narrow and quite curvy. On this particular section of the road, one blind curve was behind me and another blind curve was before me. Any car rounding either curve at the normal speed would have difficulty stopping before hitting me. Using all of my strength, I tried opening the heavy door of the older model car, but it would not budge. Instead, I hopped down from my seat and rolled down the window above me. Standing there on the glass of the passenger side window, I looked out the windshield only to see my worst fear realized…a car headed straight for me. I had no idea if the car would be able to stop, so I decided to get out as fast as possible. Pulling myself up out of the car, I jumped down from the car only to see an off-duty police officer walking toward me.

Frantic that I had just demolished my first car and confused as to what to do now that I was out, the officer suggested I go to the house on top of the embankment and call a tow truck. Too bewildered to think of tow trucks, I called my parents. They came in minutes. The owner of the house who was a friend of the family called the tow truck as I was still in shock over what had just happened. The officer went to wave traffic around the accident at the curve where the whole nightmare had begun. After my parents arrived, they decided to take me to a doctor just to make sure I was okay. Pulling out of the driveway to go to the hospital, the police officer told my dad black ice covered the road from the top to the bottom of the curve. A miracle I had survived!

Following this traumatic experience, I knew God had intervened because there was no other way to account for me walking away from that car without a scratch. I sensed God saying He wanted me to dedicate my life to serving Him. Though I was unsure of exactly what that meant, I knew I would not be alive without Him, and I immediately said yes. Slowly, I began to understand walking with God was so much more than I had known before. This experience opened up my eyes to God's miraculous power and my need to depend upon Him rather than on myself.

More Beyond Salvation

When we come to Christ for salvation, Christ's blood is what atones for our sins and makes us right before God – or the doctrinal term of justification. In Romans, Paul explained this process, *"But God demonstrates His own love toward us, in that while we were still sinners, Christ died for us. Much more then, having now been justified by His blood, we shall be saved from wrath through Him"* (Rom. 5:8-9). Many people stay in this place of salvation and do not move any further in their walk with God. They have been justified, and they are satisfied there. But if they are truly pursuing Christ and following His Word, they are confronted with a contradiction...I am a Christian who has been forgiven, and yet I still sin.

We must put off our old self referring to our sin nature. Our self-will, our self-righteousness, our self-ambition, our whole self must die on the cross. It is only in this place of being willing to die to self that we can begin to live for God. Brokenness is crucifying this "old self" so that we can become the "new creation" Christ is calling us to be.

What Is Brokenness?

Brokenness is the entry point into a deeper life with God. Indeed, brokenness does not sound like the happy Christian life many churches promise for those who are saved. Many Christians pass by this open door because it seems too difficult or requires too much of their personal sacrifice without promising enough reward for their efforts. Jesus offers everyone an invitation to come with Him into the place of deep intimacy, but He does not mandate our willingness or participation. Jesus is a gentleman who will knock but not force the door open. He will not force us to do something we do not want to do. He is faithful to show us what we need to do, but the response is up to us.

The way of Jesus often seems opposite to what the world would say is the right course of action. Most of the world is looking for a quick fix or the road that leads to the most money or popularity. Instead, He leads us in the path that will in the end produce the greatest amount of fruitfulness. His ways do not conform to the path of least resistance or the most convenient or painless process. He is most concerned that people are wholly committed to Him, His plans and His purposes. He wants to root out those things that are preventing us from having abandoned devotion in our lives.

Searching and Sifting by the Spirit

The prophet Jeremiah described the condition of our hearts, *"The heart is deceitful above all things and desperately wicked. Who can know it?"* (Jeremiah 17:9). If our hearts are in such a terrible state, how can we ever hope to be wholly like God? Jeremiah answered the question for us, *"I, the Lord, search the heart. I test the mind, even to give every man according to His ways, according to the fruit of his doings"* (Jer. 17:9-10). We have to rely upon His Holy Spirit to come, search and bring us to the place of full surrender before Him. As we allow Jesus to sift out our sin and self-life, we become more sensitive to His leading and have more room for the operation of the Spirit in our lives.

The prophet Ezekiel described this process, *"I will give you a new heart and put a new spirit within you; I will take the heart of stone out of your flesh and give you a heart of flesh. I will put My Spirit within you and cause you to walk in My statutes and you will keep My judgments and do them"* (Ezek. 36:26-27). The Lord comes to search us and cleanse us of sin. As we surrender to the brokenness, yielding to the Spirit as He breaks old habits and transforms us, we receive a new heart. A heart that no longer clings to sin. A heart of flesh that clings to the Spirit.

Brokenness is a willingness to be crushed by God. It is a painful process, but it is the way by which we find healing, wholeness and fruitfulness. Imagine a winepress: The grapes are thrust into the press, and then crushed. The way they come out is completely different than how they went in. Grapes become wine. This is how Paul described us becoming "new creations" (2 Cor. 5:17). The old form of the grapes is gone. We cannot make wine into grapes. But God, as we recognize and internalize the work of the cross, makes us into a new creation, wine.

The process of allowing God to crush the old self is a painful process. The Spirit will highlight what is hindering us from wholehearted surrender. Each time the Spirit reveals some of our old self, we have the opportunity to embrace surrender and see the Lord pour out new wine in that area of our lives. Becoming a new creation is not a once-and-done process but a continual surrender of deeper areas the Lord wants to fully control in our lives. The process of surrender allows a new wine to flow from that area.

Being Emptied Out

Another way to describe the process of brokenness is being "emptied out." The first commandment given to Moses on Mount Sinai is, *"You shall have no other gods before Me"* (Exodus 20:3). Thus, it is no surprise in Christ's new covenant that the same rules apply. If we truly want to go deep with God, we must empty out all of the things we hold higher than Jesus. This seems at first glance to be rather easy in its application. We read through the Old Testament of all of the idols other peoples worshipped and look around us, thinking to ourselves, "None of those here; check that off the list." We read about pagan altars set up to give offerings to other gods and look around us, thinking to ourselves, "None of those here; check that off the list." We think of golden idols found in other religions around the world today and look around us, "None of those here; check."

But the root of having other gods in our lives is not just about idols and altars we can see. Jesus explains that, in His Kingdom, loving anything more than Him is absolutely intolerable. Before He sent them out, Jesus told the 12 disciples, *"He who loves father or mother more than Me is not worthy of Me. And he who loves son or daughter more than Me is not worthy of Me"* (Matthew 10:37). These are usually the most important people in our lives, providing we have had good relationships with them. Jesus is not saying here we should not love our parents or children. But Jesus is saying nothing can stand in the way of our love and obedience to Him. Jesus Himself lived by this same principle. In Luke 8, we read of Jesus' mother, Mary, and his brothers when they came to see Him. Jesus does not change His course of ministry to bend to the will of His family. Doing the will of the Father was His first priority. Therefore, part of following Jesus is choosing not to love people more than God. We cannot allow family to determine our decisions in life or ministry. Our first priority must be to obey the will of God.

Our security does not rest with our families. This is good news for those who come from broken homes where family is not such a great word. For those who come from strong families, this may be more of a cross to bear. Christ calls us to lay down anything hindering us from fully giving our lives to Him. He wants complete control. If our decision to say "yes" to God's calling rests with whether our parents will approve, then we have our priorities out of order. Jesus is telling us He will have no one else who comes before Him. This is tricky for some cultures where honoring parents is held in highest regard. However, we must recognize if Christ's Kingdom and this world are opposed to one another, our choice is always Christ's way.

Another sinister desire that can creep into our hearts if we are not careful is the love of money. In the Sermon on the Mount, Jesus explains in repeated illustrations our treasure must be Christ alone and being conformed into His image. Sometimes, we try to blur the lines to make the gospel more acceptable, but Jesus is very clear. Jesus said, *"No one can serve two masters; for either he will hate the one and love the other, or else he will be loyal to the one and despise the other. You cannot serve God and mammon"* (Matthew 6:24). This statement does not say that if one is rich, he or she cannot serve God. Jesus is talking about money having sway over our hearts. This can be true of rich and poor alike. When we make decisions related to the call of God on our lives based on money, we have made money the master of our destiny.

In rooting out the love of money, we still need to be wise stewards with the resources God has given to each one. Jesus is not telling us to throw away common sense. He is not telling us to make foolish investments. He is telling us money cannot be the determining factor for whether we say "yes" to God. If God has called us, then He will supply and we can trust His bank account will never run dry. In the Sermon on the Mount, Jesus goes on to talk about worry related to finances. If we are worrying, then money is still the master. If we are resting and trusting Jesus, God is truly Lord of our lives.

The sin of the self-life is filled with opportunities for us to bear the cross: whether we are trapped by the love of self, loving ourselves and our ways more than God; or self-ambition, seeking after what will move us further along in our career or in our status in society; or self-righteousness, thinking we are okay on our own and do not need God's help in this area or that area; or self-help, having a problem and figuring out a way to fix it on your own. These areas of our life must be crucified for the life of Jesus to transform how to love ourselves—which is God's ambition for our lives, understanding righteousness comes through Jesus' blood alone and not by our own effort and truly experiencing a dependence on the Lord to help us through circumstances we cannot fix on our own. God is challenging us to go beyond ourselves. He is making available to us His very power, His love, His righteousness,

His Spirit to help us, and His enabling grace to overcome; but unless we are willing to die to ourselves we will never experience what He has made available to us. Truly embracing our weakness is the only way to experience the resurrection power of Christ's strength inside of us.

In this place of dying to self, we do not lose our own identity. God is not asking us to become someone different than who we are, but He is asking us to become the greatest potential of who He intended us to become. The first step to dying to our flesh is recognizing we are created by God with a spirit, mind and body. Our temptation in life is to live and make choices based on what we think with our mind or feel with our body because these things are tangible realities. However, when we become Christians, our choices are now to be based upon the Spirit of God.

Many times, we limit this understanding of "denying ourselves" to practical actions such as not doing drugs, not saying certain things, being careful about what we watch with our eyes, etc. However, God's goal for us to become more like His Son is not contained solely nor primarily in the things that we do but in who we are becoming. Therefore, dying to our flesh and the choices we are asked to make for Christ are also centered around our attitudes and responses to people. When someone says something that is not true and hurts our feelings, do we respond in anger and lash out? Or do we choose meekness and not respond in kind? This is the process by which Christ is engaging our nature and helping us choose responses that align with His heart.

The Other Junk

As we say "yes" to God emptying out those things that are not like Jesus, we enter into a process where God searches through our lives and empties out all of the sin and junk that has built up. We have overlooked some heart issues or refused to deal with them at the time. Maybe we have had some hard experiences we never processed, and we just moved on without understanding what God was doing in those circumstances. We have harbored these for years, unwilling to give them to Jesus.

Often, we have unforgiveness and bitterness we have been storing for a rainy day. It is kind of messy business, so we do not really want to deal with it. Not wanting to dredge up old memories or painful circumstances, we sweep it under the rug in hopes it will disappear. Other junk is hidden sin we are very good at keeping from others. It is easy to develop areas of weakness where we know our responses are wrong, but it is too hard to stop.

Now that we see we all have junk, let's imagine a huge room filled with boxes of every shape and size from the floor to the ceiling, so much so that one cannot even enter the room. If we want to get into that room, we have to sort through the boxes, remove the junk. This huge room is like our heart. The moment we come to faith, it is so filled with sin that Jesus barely has enough room to fit. As the Holy Spirit shows us or reminds us of things, we must confess, repent and ask for help to walk in a new way. Some of the boxes will leave with a single prayer and the victory is ours. However, other boxes are not as easy to remove.

One lady who came to me was a leader in Christian ministry who had been hurt repeatedly by another leader. She told me the Lord had brought this man to mind, and she had forgiven him for the hurt he had caused her. But she said she still felt a cringe in her stomach when she would even think of the man. I told her forgiveness is rarely a one-time event. Forgiveness is a process by which the boxes of hurt, anger, unforgiveness, bitterness and anything else is removed from our heart.

But walking this out step by step allows our emotions to catch up to the reality in the spiritual realm. Every time we think of that person, we release forgiveness over them. Every time we see them in the market, we release forgiveness over them silently if we have already spoken the words to them before. Over and over, we bless them in the spirit of forgiveness until our emotions finally catch up to what we have been saying. As these boxes of sin are removed through the process of forgiveness, Jesus comes in a greater measure to fill us with Himself.

We wait on God, and when He is ready to remove the box, He will give us the power to release forgiveness and walk into the healing and freedom He wants to pour into us.

Confession is a powerful tool available to us through the Spirit. The confession of our sin to the Father is absolutely necessary. Until we are ready to call it sin, we can never receive the grace to overcome it. Confession enables us to verbalize what we know to be true and then practice it. We know in our hearts something is sin, but until we have verbalized this to the Lord, we will continue to feel the condemnation of the enemy. Confessing our sins brings it into the light and cuts off the power of the enemy. Similarly, once we have identified the sin, confessing with our mouths the truth of forgiveness over another person or situation releases power to overcome it. We know we have forgiven the person, but unless we continue to confess it we can slip into doubt. Through confession, power is released to see us walk in the freedom Christ intended for us. We confess what we know to be true, not what we feel, and in the process what we feel will become what is true.

We cannot let our emotions dictate our spirituality. This is a common problem that will easily lead us off course. Our emotions do not determine if we are saved. Jesus' blood answers that question. Our emotions do not determine whether to obey God's will. Our will determines our obedience. Even though we feel one way does not mean that we need to act on those feelings. In fact, often in the Christian life our emotions do not lead us into the decision, but we will find joy after we have obeyed. We must draw a line in the sand to say no to the culture around us that would want to have our emotions determine our destiny. God's calling goes far beyond and often in opposite directions to the way of our emotions. In choosing the way of brokenness, we lay down our emotions and choose to act on what we know to be true.

The Reality of Forgiveness

Forgiveness is a major part of the gospel. Sometimes, forgiveness is overlooked as the thing we do when we first come to salvation. But, in reality, forgiveness is a critical part to *the abandoned devotion lifestyle.* Forgiveness is promised to us by God: *"If we confess our sins, He is faithful and just to forgive us our sins and to cleanse us from all unrighteousness"* (1 John 1:9). Forgiveness is the basis for our relationship with Christ, and it is also the tool we use to continue to move forward in life with Christ.

We live in a broken world, full of broken human beings. We can be tricked into thinking when we go to church, we will find a perfect world because they are all Christians. But the truth is no matter how far we have gone in our sanctification, it is not complete until we reach heaven. We will continue to hurt others, most times unintentionally, but forgiveness still needs to cover those situations. We can continue to offer forgiveness to others no matter how many times they have hurt us because of the grace and forgiveness we have received from Christ. We love and forgive because He first loved and forgave us.

We see the special emphasis Jesus brings to forgiveness in the Sermon on the Mount. Not only do we see forgiveness in the Lord's prayer (Matthew 6:12), but He immediately repeats and expands upon this in verses 14 and 15. Forgiveness is essential to moving deeper with God. Through prayer, we unleash the power of forgiveness not only over our relationships with other people but also in our relationship with God. Jesus gives a direct correlation between our forgiveness of others and our relationship with God. If we want to be close to God, then we need to forgive others, and the sooner the easier. If we do not forgive others, our relationship with God is blocked and we lose the intimacy we once had.

Forgiveness breaks the power of the enemy. Forgiveness lies in direct opposition to the resentment and bitterness the enemy loves to sow among the children of God. In the Sermon on the Mount,

Jesus highlights as one of the beatitudes the necessity of possessing the quality of being "pure in heart" (Matthew 5:8). While some have interpreted this beatitude to reflect upon our personal relationship with the Lord when we come to faith, this beatitude also has a much deeper meaning. The beatitudes are building on one another, and the second half of the beatitudes–the last four–are all focused outward in relationship with other people. The "pure in heart" are those who walk in purity of heart with others. This is a real area of struggle if we are easily offended or harbor bitterness and unforgiveness toward others. The power of forgiveness enables believers to walk in purity of heart before the Lord, not in a once-and-done kind of way, but by continually laying down offenses and picking up the cross of forgiveness as Jesus did when He said, *"Father, forgive them, for they know not what they do"* (Luke 23:34).

Costly Devotion

The abandoned devotion Christ calls us to possess is costly. We have already seen how His lordship requires that He is loved and obeyed before all others. But when we are emptied out in brokenness before God, we are shown our deep weaknesses. Satan comes to tempt us, but God comes to test us and show us our weaknesses so our hearts can be completely His.

In the life of Job, we see a man whom God allowed to be tested. Everything Job held dear in life is stripped away from him. His children died; his possessions are destroyed; his very life itself was attacked with illness. The world would say "Enough! There is no reason left to live." But Job was a man who had cultivated a lifestyle of abandoned devotion. He would not curse God as his wife encouraged him to do. He knew God loved him, even though his whole world was crashing around him. His circumstances did not determine his worth or success or identity. God wanted Job to come to the end of himself so he could see his desperate need for God. This is brokenness, realizing our desperate need for God no matter what the cost. Job embraced the opportunity to know God in a deeper way. He ran to God and not away from Him.

The costliness of our devotion can sometimes be taken for granted. The Israelites ran into this problem, and the prophet Malachi was sent to set things right. The Israelites had taken God for granted. They knew they were the covenant people and that God loved them. But instead of letting the truth of God's love produce love and obedience in their hearts, they began to cut corners. They turned God's covenantal love into cheap grace saying "We are God's people so we can do whatever we want, and God will still love us." They still offered sacrifices as was expected, but they did not give their very best, which would have actually cost them. They gave the worthless animals they could not sell anyway – the blind, lame and sick. They refused to give God what would shrink their bottom line. In other words, profit became more important than God. God would have none of it. He told them if they thought it was okay to give the worthless animals as an offering, then try giving it to the governor. (Mal. 1)

Our status as God's beloved sons and daughters does not entitle us to give less. We cannot cut corners with God's requirements. He must be our highest priority and our greatest goal—anything less is sin. When our thoughts begin to look for ways to avoid the cost, we know something else is gripping our hearts. We need to turn inward and see what the Holy Spirit is highlighting in our hearts. God's everlasting love should buoy us up when the cost becomes great. His fervent love for us should cause us to reach higher and deeper toward having the fullness of God in us.

For some Christians who have walked with God for many years, there may be a temptation to settle into a routine of activities but lose the dynamic relationship God desires. We cannot let familiarity creep into our walk with God and steal the joy of being delighted in His presence and the testimony of His faithfulness throughout our lives. Familiarity can breed complacency which allows those little foxes to gain a greater foothold in our lives.

God is committed to the process of stripping away everything we use as a crutch to prop ourselves up, other than God alone. He wants us completely for Himself. He wants us passionately pursuing His presence whether we are 20 or 60 years old. He is jealous of our time spent on other things when we do not make time for Him; He is jealous of our love when we give it to others and not to Him; He is jealous of our affections when we are joyful in serving others but not in serving Him; He is jealous of our money when we use it on ourselves and do not give it to whom He has asked. In taking these things away, we see the costliness of our devotion. Choosing to walk the way of the cross, the way of brokenness, means we must surrender all.

Our brokenness can also be costly in other ways. Sometimes, sin requires restitution. Some of the things we have done in the past require not only forgiveness but a token to show our deep repentance. Take the story of Zacchaeus, for example. Zacchaeus, a chief tax collector, was rich and wanted to see Jesus. Because of his short stature, he climbed a tree to get a better view. Jesus came by, saw him and said he wanted to come to his house. Zacchaeus ran ahead to make preparations, joyfully. Once Jesus came, he sat talking with Zacchaeus in his house. Finally, the truth became clear and Zacchaeus stood and said to Jesus, *"'Look, Lord, I give half of my goods to the poor; and if I have taken anything from anyone by false accusation. I restore fourfold.' And Jesus said to him, 'Today salvation has come to this house, because he also is a son of Abraham; for the Son of Man has come to seek and to save that which was lost'"* (Luke 19:1-10).

Part of responding to the gospel through abandoned devotion is to count Jesus more worthy than anything else. Zacchaeus understood this. In contrast to the rich young ruler, he gladly gave away half his possessions and restored fourfold to all from whom he had deceitfully stolen. The Law of Moses commanded that one restore what had been taken and add one-fifth to it. Zacchaeus was not merely trying to abide by a law, but he had truly seen the error of his ways, and coming in the opposite spirit gave far beyond what was required. His heart had been set free from the power of greed and lust for money. He now saw Jesus as Abraham had, his *"shield and exceedingly great reward"* (Gen. 15:1).

King David also understood the costliness of abandoned devotion. He had taken a census of the army, which revealed the sin of depending upon men and numbers rather than on God's leading and strength. As soon as he had taken the census, his heart condemned him and immediately he turned to God in repentance. The prophet Gad came to announce God's punishment for David's sin. Because of God's graciousness, He allowed David to choose his punishment, and David chose to fall into the hand of the Lord and have a plague cover the land for three days. The cost was severe–70,000 men died because of the plague. But David knew the God whom he served, so he built an altar before the Lord to pray for the plague to be withdrawn from the people. He went to the property of Araunah the Jebusite to buy his threshing floor and the oxen for the sacrifice. Araunah wanted to give freely the things which the king requested. But David understood real repentance will cost us something. David said to Araunah, *"No, but I will surely buy it from you for a price; nor will I offer burnt offerings to the Lord my God with that which costs me nothing"* (2 Sam. 24:24).

When confronted with our sin, we must turn to Jesus immediately. Our first thought cannot be to run away or forget about it. God does not point out our sin because He is cruel and enjoys watching us suffer for our mistakes. His kindness and love desire us to be in constant fellowship with Him, and sin disrupts that fellowship. His grace and mercy cause Him to intervene. He reveals our sin so we can turn to Him in repentance and restore our relationship with Him. This restoration comes with the price of humbling ourselves. The greatest enemy to our relationship with God is ourselves, our pride, self-righteousness, self-sufficiency, self-pity, and selfish ambition. Those who choose *the abandoned devotion lifestyle* must be willing to pay the price of dying to self. These are the same terms Jesus gave to those who followed Him, *"If anyone desires to come after Me, let him deny himself, and take up his cross daily, and follow Me"* (Luke 9:23). Being a true follower of Jesus means denying one's self and taking up one's cross. This is *the abandoned devotion lifestyle.*

Brokenness Produces Love and Devotion

The cost of having our pride stripped away, relinquishing the dependence upon self and the abilities of our flesh, choosing to humble ourselves before God is painful. Though painful, His ways produce love and devotion in our hearts. It is only as we truly come to grips with the depths of our weakness and inability to save ourselves that we see the glorious power of God flowing through us.

The apostle Paul testified of this in his own life, *"And He [the Lord] said to me, 'My grace is sufficient for you, for My strength is made perfect in weakness.' Therefore, most gladly I will rather boast in my infirmities, that the power of Christ may rest upon me. Therefore, I take pleasure in infirmities, in reproaches, in needs, in persecutions, in distresses, for Christ's sake. For when I am weak, then I am strong"* (2 Corinthians 12:9-10). Paul understood the mystery of God filling us with Himself. When our pride and self-sufficiency rise up in a situation, we have no room for God to operate in us. But when we confess our weakness in a situation and cry out to God for help, He rushes in and shows His glorious strength. Therefore, Paul writes that he does not run away from difficulties but instead takes pleasure in them because he expects God to show up.

A beautiful picture of our brokenness producing love and devotion is Jesus being anointed by a woman whose sins were known to all and yet had been forgiven and set free by Jesus. She came to Jesus, fully grasping her brokenness and desperate need for Him. She came joyfully to pour out a blessing on the One who had set her free. She poured out the costly devotion of an alabaster jar of fragrant oil. She did not care about the others who would mock her. She did not heed their taunts and jeers. She came out of love. Jesus, seeing this woman and hearing their words, decided to help them understand by telling them a parable of a creditor and two debtors—one who owed 500 denarii and the other 50. The creditor forgives both, and Jesus asks which one loves more. Even the mockers agreed, the one to whom more was forgiven.

The depth of our brokenness corresponds to greater love being poured into our hearts. We are all sinners; not one of us is better than any other. When this understanding of brokenness goes deeper in our hearts, greater love for Jesus flows out of us. It is this love that leads us into wholehearted devotion.

Contemplation:

A good gauge of how you are doing in surrendering your self-life is to reflect on your responses to God and to others. When God asks you to do something, do you immediately give excuses? When someone asks you to do something for them, do you try to get out of it or do you do it because it will make you look good? When someone brings up something that is critical of you, a defensive response often indicates there is pride and a lack of humility and meekness in that area.

What are areas that the Lord is highlighting to you? God is not asking for perfection today. He is asking us to begin the process in the area that He is highlighting to us. He is asking us to go deeper and embrace Him in new ways. He is asking us to let go of more of ourselves in order for His life in us to flourish and grow.

1. What is something of brokenness that you need for the Lord to take to a deeper level in your being? Often, we have all heard this before, but each time we hear it the Lord will highlight some part where He wants to give us greater revelation. Ask the Lord for more living understanding in the area He is highlighting to you.

2. Moving further in this movement of brokenness, what is something the Lord is highlighting for you to share with someone else? The Lord does not just give truth to us for our own encouragement, but He opens our eyes to truth in order to help set others free with these same keys. Share the keys! Open the doors!

Prayer:

Lord Jesus, I dedicate my whole self to you again and declare over my life that You are Lord. I ask you, Holy Spirit, to come and search my heart. Show me the areas You want to remove by the power of the cross. Give me power in my spirit to say "yes" to you and to continually walk in an attitude of surrender. I want to grow deeper, and I don't want anything to hinder my walk with You. Release power to choose the costliness of obedience and say yes. In Jesus' name, AMEN.

3

Cultivating Intimacy
Walking in Love

Glimpses of grace abound in the Word of God as we see the unfolding of God's plan to give His own Son so we might be fully His. In the *abandoned devotion lifestyle*, our goal is to become people who are fully conformed to the image of Christ. This conforming process begins in the place of brokenness but moves us toward intimacy. God wants us to be emptied out so He can fill us with more of Himself.

As we set out on this journey of knowing more of who Christ calls us to be, we see our life in God is centered around the death and resurrection of Christ. In embracing the fullness of the cross, we can enter into the fullness of life in the resurrection with Him. In the words of Paul, *"that I may gain Christ and be found in him, ... that I may know Him and the power of His resurrection, and the fellowship of His sufferings, being conformed to His death, if by any means, I may attain to the resurrection from the dead"* (Philippians 3:9-11). We experience the brokenness and death in order to have the fullness of the resurrection power living inside of us.

The cross, death and resurrection to which we refer here are not merely a transformation that takes place when we receive Christ or when we are baptized and raised to new life. Neither does the fullness of the cross, death and resurrection happen by God's sovereignty in the Christian life. Rather, we must choose to enter into the sufferings of our Lord through the cross. We must choose to die with Him; not our mortal bodies, but crucifying our flesh nature. And we must choose to grow into His beloved Bride by His resurrection power flowing out of ourselves through the choices we make, the words we speak, and the actions we take.

Dietrich Bonhoeffer, a famous theologian who died for his faith in a Nazi concentration camp, wrote a letter to his students in August 1941 in which he explains the mysterious connection between death and life. Many of his students had already died in the war, and his words here were intended to bring comfort to those grieving for their brethren. His words also foreshadow the very experience that awaited him a few short years later. He writes,

> In life with Jesus Christ, death as a general fate approaching from without is confronted by death from within, one's own death, the free death of daily dying with Jesus Christ. Those who live with Christ die daily to their own will. Christ in us gives us over to death so that he can live within us. Thus, our inner dying grows to meet that death from without. Christians receive their own death in this way, and in this way our physical death very truly comes not the end but rather the fulfillment of our life with Jesus Christ. [3]

Our life in Christ is inexplicably connected to our willingness to die daily. For Bonhoeffer, the "death without" was becoming an ever-increasing reality, but he saw his dying daily inside was preparing him for his mortal death. Here in this inner dying, he found a freedom was released to embrace the fullness of God. This same reality is what Paul describes in Galatians.

In the book of Galatians, Paul has been speaking to them of how they have turned away from the one true gospel to embrace another that is false. They have exchanged a dependence upon grace and faith in God for a dependence upon themselves and their own flesh. In exhorting them, he wants to help them understand that the flesh, or what Bonhoeffer termed "our own will," is in opposition to Christ. To live wholeheartedly for Christ, we must first be crucified with Christ. He wrote, "*I have been crucified with Christ and I no longer live, but Christ lives in me. The life I live in the flesh I live by faith in the Son of God who loved me and gave Himself for me*" (Galatians 2:20).

Living from the place of crucifixion is a daily choice to live from the place of not "I" but "Christ." This is a very practical reality for living with wholehearted devotion. From the place of brokenness in our surrender, we can choose to live single-mindedly toward Christ. Saying "no" to the flesh also means saying "yes" to God. Each time we are presented with even seemingly good things, God has His best desire for us in that circumstance. Our willingness to say "no" to the flesh opens up space for saying "yes" to God. Our choices matter. Each choice has consequences that either lead us closer to God or further away from Him.

The Holy Spirit As Our Helper

God has given us a key to help us in this process of becoming single-minded. The Holy Spirit is our Helper who is here to guide us in the process of becoming more like Jesus. Paul writes that it is necessity for followers of Jesus to "walk according to the Spirit" and "not according to the flesh" (Romans 8). The transition from our old way of making decisions based upon our flesh to a new way based on the leading of the Spirit can be difficult. How do we know it is the Spirit or our flesh? The choices of the Spirit lead us closer to God. They are not always easy choices, as often the road God chooses is rooted in humility and meekness, but we will always have the peace of God in our spirit when we choose what God is asking of us. The ways of the flesh usually come from wrong attitudes and sometimes from emotional highs or lows.

As a follower of Jesus, we know when we have made a decision based upon our flesh instead of the Spirit because we have an unsettled feeling, no peace from God. If we are provoked by a lack of peace, the best resolution is to go do what God was asking as quickly as possible, even if it means looking bad or having to go back on what was said. Our quick obedience to the Lord will restore our fellowship with Him that was broken by our disobedience. As we grow in our sensitivity to the Spirit, we more accurately discern God's leading.

Our level of surrender will determine our experience of intimacy with Christ. Often, I hear people who want to jump right into intimacy with God without talking about surrender. But we must surrender an area to the Lord before we can begin to see God move in that area of our life. If we have not surrendered our ambitions and dreams, then the Lord will not speak to us about His purposes and plans for our lives. If we have not surrendered our finances, then we cannot expect God to move in supernatural ways related to finances. The direct correlation between surrender and intimacy must drive us back to surrender because we are desperate for more intimacy. As we experience greater intimacy, we see the joy that comes from surrender. Slowly, we release more and more to the Lord. If we do not see the connection, we will remain in a shallow place of intimacy because we have not surrendered to the Lord.

Saying 'No' in Order to Say 'YES!'

We read in the gospels the story of Mary, the sister of Lazarus and Martha, who made the choice on three different occasions to be single-minded and say "no" to other opportunities in order to say "yes" to Jesus. She is a faithful witness of what wholehearted devotion really means. When we choose to move closer to God, He also moves closer to us (James 4:8). This movement of choosing one another develops a joyful intimacy producing extravagant devotion.

Mary first met Jesus when He was out teaching in her village of Bethany. Martha welcomed Him into their home, and Mary sat with the disciples at Jesus' feet and listened to His words. She was captivated with His teaching. Her heart was pricked by the deep truth Jesus was sharing with them. She did not offer to help Martha in the kitchen as she labored to feed Jesus and His disciples. Feeling like Mary was neglecting her duty, Martha implored Jesus for Mary to get off the ground and into the kitchen to help her. Jesus responded, *"Martha, Martha, you are worried and troubled about many things. But one thing is needed, and Mary has chosen that good part, which will not be taken away from her"* (Luke 10:41-42).

Martha was fixated on her problem of needing to serve these men and could not see beyond her personal circumstances. Jesus explains to Martha that He understands her troubles and worries, but there is a time and place for everything. Mary has chosen correctly right now to sit and listen. Mary and Martha would have had time later for cleaning up the kitchen. Serving was not bad. Jesus does not condemn Martha. He simply tells her there are certain times for certain things, and we must make the most of every moment. Our priorities will determine how we spend those moments. Mary's choice was for the good thing at that moment. Martha could have laid down her work for a while and sat with the others listening to Jesus. We put pressure and a burden on ourselves that Jesus has not asked us to carry. Jesus is offering freedom even to Martha to see there is another way. Martha did not feel she had the freedom to choose, but Jesus is saying, "YES! You have the freedom to choose just as Mary did. You have that same freedom."

Martha succumbed to the pressures around her, whether it was the cultural norm for women to be in the kitchen serving the men during a meal, the pressure of pleasing other people, or a need to be busy in order to be successful. The number of pressures around us can leave us feeling as if we do not have a choice, but that is a lie. No matter how many pressures we have, we always have a choice. God is waiting with arms outstretched for us to come and meet with Him, if we will only take the time and make the choice.

Our choices reflect our priorities. As we prioritize what Jesus called the first commandment of loving God with all our heart, soul, mind and strength, we make choices reflecting our commitment to pursue it (Matthew 22:37). Mike Bickle writes, "The gazing heart of devotion is the primary thing that sets everything else in motion in the divine order."[4] Our choice to behold Him brings order to our life. It orders our priorities and brings us in line with God's heart. Mary chose to gaze upon Jesus and be transformed by His presence. This is our choice today – to choose to behold Him. But this choice often comes at the price of choosing it before or instead of something else. We will become what we behold. If our choices give in to the flesh, then we begin beholding those things that lead us away from Jesus. But as we continue to say "yes" to Jesus and spend time in His presence, we will be transformed into His image (2 Corinthians 3:18).

Choosing to behold Him brings us to the place of intimacy. The hardest part of intimacy is that it takes time. Over and over again, we have to make the choice to spend time in His presence. We have to choose to be patient and wait. Sometimes, our time with God can seem dry when we may not have a special sense of His presence. But we do not give up and walk away. We keep doing what God commands us to do. We read His Word and meditate upon it day and night. We worship the Lord in the Spirit and celebrate with adoration His matchless grace. We recount the wonderful deeds He has done in our lives in the past. This is the first step toward intimacy, choosing wisely to press into Jesus, spending time in His presence, and reading His Word.

Building Relationship–Confidence in God

Mary's second encounter with Jesus is when her brother Lazarus becomes sick, and Mary and Martha send a message to Jesus to inform Him. John describes the special relationship Jesus had with Mary, Martha and Lazarus as one of deep love for them (John 11:5). The Scriptures do not record many other instances where Jesus loved a particular person. This family held a special place in his heart, where

He could sense their devotion to Him. Later, we will see Jesus had such fond affection for this family that He returns to their home before His crucifixion.

Here, we see Mary's confidence in Jesus' ability to heal her brother. Out of her time spent listening to Jesus' teaching and seeing Him perform miracles, her relationship grows into a confident trust in the character and power of Jesus. She and Martha sent word to Jesus that Lazarus was sick. Notice Mary and Martha did not ask Him to come, they only told Him Lazarus was sick. Doubtless, Mary had seen Jesus heal people by merely speaking the words. He did not have to lay hands on Lazarus in order for him to be healed. Jesus needed only to speak the words. But Jesus had a greater plan than what Mary and Martha could see.

Instead of going to see Lazarus or speaking the words of his healing, Jesus chooses to continue doing ministry in the same place for two more days. Upon coming to Bethany, Martha runs out to meet Jesus and questions His delay in coming, allowing Lazarus to die. Martha's interaction with Jesus is filled with faith in Jesus' ability, yet from a distance of knowing truths. Mary stays waiting at the house. She is confident Jesus will come even though Lazarus has died. And at the moment Martha tells her Jesus has come, she runs to Him. Bowing low in humility before her Lord and weeping over her brother, she asks Jesus why He did not come sooner. She repeats the exact words of Martha, but Jesus' response is to groan in the Spirit. Her tears and the weeping of all her friends who had followed her moved Jesus' heart with compassion. He knew why He had waited, but the reality of seeing His friend in pain still grieved His heart.

This moment between Jesus and Mary reveals the deep intimacy they had developed. They were not just talking about truths but sharing the real emotions of pain. When we have cultivated this intimacy with Jesus, our hurts move Jesus' heart, and in the same way those things that bring pain to the heart of the Father move us to pray. David understood this kind of intimacy. In the Psalms, he pours out everything in his heart to God – his hurts, frustrations and failures as well as the joy, praise and adoration. He knew God could handle all of it and help him to work through it to come to what God was saying in the midst of the situation. Our intimacy with God not only helps us to share our experiences with God, but it also invites us to share in what is on God's heart. As we listen to what the Spirit is saying, we hear the things on the heart of the Father. This leads us to deeper intimacy with God where it is less and less about the things on our heart and more what is on the heart of the Father.

This is the second part of intimacy, where we build relationship with God, and we develop a two-way communication with the Father, sharing heart to heart. This same principle applies to relationships between people. The first stages of a relationship are often very superficial. But the more time we spend with another person, the more we share from our hearts. As we are reading His Word, we gain more understanding of His ways and His heart. Our relationship grows into a partnership where God wants us to help accomplish the plans and purposes on His heart. We also develop confidence through this building of relationship—confidence in hearing His voice, and confidence in His ability and desire to act.

Hearing God's Voice

One thing we all crave as followers of Jesus is to hear the voice of God. Whether we want to hear God speaking to us to know we matter to Him or because we are seeking direction in our lives, we all want to hear God speaking to us. Our earnest desire to hear God's voice is a vital part of our relationship with God. The problem most of us have is thinking the voice of God is going to be audible or even flashing neon lights.

Sometimes, God speaks to non-Christians to turn their hearts toward Him or reveal something important. However, they are not always aware it is God speaking to them. But, as children of God we are His sheep, and He promises we will know and can hear His voice (John

10:1-5). God speaking to us is not only a general sense of knowing but also a specific instance of hearing specific words. Sometimes, we ask questions like, "What does His voice sound like? How can I learn to hear His voice? If the Lord is speaking to me, then why don't I hear Him?" These are common questions as we grow in our relationship with the Lord.

First Steps: Learning to Recognize His Voice

In order to hear the voice of God, we have to learn the ways God speaks. The Lord loves us and wants to speak to us, but because we do not know what it sounds like we often miss it. Growing up, often I would go on walks through our farm with my dad. Dad would hear a bird call, and he would call back to it. They would go back and forth chattering to one another, but I was unable to enter into the dialogue because I had not learned the language. I did not even know what to listen for out in nature much less how to communicate back again. Sure, I had heard the birds chirping before, but it had all sounded the same because I could not distinguish distinct bird calls. In the same way, we may hear the words God is speaking but because we are not trained to recognize His voice we just think of it as the same things we have always heard or we think it is just our own thoughts. The God of the universe wants to speak to us, but we cannot enter into dialogue with Him unless we are able to hear and understand what He is saying.

Growing in discerning God's voice takes practice. We begin by waiting patiently in prayer, listening to what we hear, and then taking time to write it all down in a journal. Then, take what was heard and test it against the Bible. Often, God will speak to His children through the Bible. As we read the Word of God, we have certain words jump off the page, seemingly more important than the other words. This is the Holy Spirit speaking. Pray over that word or phrase and ask God what He wants to say about it. He will give pictures and impressions about what to do based upon those Scriptures. Even if the Lord does not give a specific Scripture, His words will resonate as aligning with Scripture.

There are other voices we hear when we are quiet before the Lord. Our flesh is often easily distracted by a list of things to do and pressure from other people. In order to go deeper in prayer and listening, write down the distractions and lay them to the side. At times, we might hear other voices and are not sure if it is God. Ask God to silence every other voice except His own and open your ears to hear Him clearly.

God can speak to us in many different ways. Every day as we read the Word of God, He desires that we would hear His voice highlighting certain Scriptures and speaking to us about how those Scriptures apply to our lives. He wants the words He speaks to affect the way we live. The Lord can speak through dreams and visions as we see in the life of Joseph in Genesis 37:5-9, Peter in Acts 10:9-16, or Paul in Acts 16:9-10. The Lord can also speak through angelic visitations such as with Cornelius in Acts 10:31-32 or Mary in Luke 1:28. As we are praying, the Lord may give you a Scripture that becomes a powerful weapon to bring freedom, deliverance or answer to prayer.

God can also speak through many other forms today. He can speak through movies, books or other forms of print or electronic media. The Lord can talk to us through other people or through His creation all around us. The God of the universe is not limited in how He can speak. He is only limited by what we are able to hear. Are we listening? Are we tuned in and ready for Him to speak?

It is also good to keep a journal of the ways God speaks. By writing it down, it will be easier to identify patterns in the way God speaks and make it easier to discern His voice. After seeing different patterns, it is always good to ask God to open up new ways of speaking. If there is a particular way of hearing God's voice that seems interesting, ask God to speak in that way and then wait and expect God to speak.

Training Our Ears to Hear

We must train ourselves in listening for Him to speak. Our relationship and conversation are not just about bringing our problems to Him to get His advice. We want to grow in our relationship with God so He can share what is on His heart with us. But the key is listening. Sometimes, although we can hear God's voice, we don't actively engage with God by asking Him questions and listening for His response. When we have a time of prayer and all we do is tell God everything troubling us, then we have only enjoyed half of the benefit of prayer. We have to practice listening, discerning and responding.

Often, as we are beginning to hear God speak, we bring questions to God in prayer and wait for an answer. However, as we grow, the Lord wants to begin telling us things on His heart. He wants us to align with the purposes on His heart and pray those things into being. This is the participatory part of prayer where it is not all about us and what we want, but about God revealing to us those things He wants and then agreeing with Him in intercession.

It is just like playing sports. If one wants to be a good basketball player, it takes more than just learning how to shoot the ball. We have to practice shooting, defense and listening to our teammates to be good at the game of basketball. We cannot just tell ourselves that, once we have learned to hear the voice of God, that is enough. We have to be able to distinguish His voice in times of stress, chaos and transition when many things are clamoring for our attention. If we have listened intently repeated times when not under stress, we are more able to discern the Lord speaking to us when there is a crisis in our lives. Not only are we better able to discern God's voice, but because of repeated practice and the discipline to first go and listen to the Lord, we do not immediately jump to conclusions in a situation. We are able to wait upon the Lord and discern His leading without becoming stressed and anxious because of the circumstances.

This part of hearing God's voice is the most enjoyable part of being in relationship. We spend time communing with God and listening to what He wants to say, and He gives us opportunities to affect real change in circumstances all around us. Whether for speaking words into people's lives, being sensitive to the Spirit's leading as we talk to people in the street or at the market, we have so many opportunities every day for God to work through us, but we get so wrapped up in our own agenda that we miss them. Instead, we need to wake up in the morning and ask the Lord, "Give me opportunities to speak the words on Your heart to someone else today."

If the Lord asks us to do something, we must respond in obedience. As we respond, we should experience the peace of God. Repeat this same exercise several times in order to begin discerning what is God's voice and what is the flesh or your own will. I will talk more about the importance of obedience in a later chapter.

Practicing His Presence

As we are listening to hear God's voice, we must consistently practice being in His presence throughout the day. We cannot limit God to our time in the morning in prayer and Bible study if we really want to grow in intimacy with the Lord. We have to be people who are constantly communing with God throughout our day.

In Exodus, we read the story of Moses in the wilderness with the Israelites. Having already gone through many experiences in the wilderness, including the incident with the golden calf, Moses is acutely aware of his need for God in order to lead these people to the Promised Land. His only hope is in God going with him and providing for the Israelites in the wilderness. As Moses meets with God, he says to the Lord, "If Your Presence does not go with us, do not bring us up from here" (Exodus 33:15). Moses is in essence saying that he is not going anywhere unless God goes with him.

Moses understood the necessity of living in God's presence and constantly pursuing a deeper level of intimacy on a regular basis. He was not content for God to speak only occasionally until arriving in the Promised Land. Then, as Moses presses into God for more of His presence, God reveals to Moses His glory. God will reward our pursuit of Him with a greater revelation and understanding of Himself.

This awakening to God's presence in the midst of our lives is not just a general sense of God with us. We can practice interacting with His presence throughout the day. Brother Lawrence commented, "There is no sweeter manner of living in the world than continuous communion with God."[5] In the morning, we say good morning to the Holy Spirit and invite Him into our day. We do not limit our prayer times to when we sit and read the Bible but rather lay hold of little moments here and there throughout the day to talk to him. The goal is to be in continuous fellowship with the Lord throughout the day; every activity, every task, asking the Lord for help and then praising Him for His help and goodness.

In my personal walk with the Lord, I find moments while driving here or there to talk to the Lord and ask Him what is on His heart; or while I am washing dishes, I ask the Lord to come and cleanse my heart and show me what things inside of me need to be washed in the blood of Christ. There are also times while getting ready in the morning or taking a shower that I will quiet my heart and just listen. When I have something hard to do, I ask the Lord for strength and wisdom. Afterwards, I give thanks for the Lord's grace. The practice of gratitude for all of the seemingly small things we experience as God's intervening hand helps to create a habit of thanksgiving and praise in our hearts. This remembrance of God's works in our lives produces thanksgiving that in turn produces joy.

Over the years, I have listened as the Lord has spoken deep and insightful words to me, things I never would have heard had I not been tuned into the Spirit and actively seeking and waiting on the Lord in prayer. This is a discipline that we will not master in a day, and I still have not mastered it. However, we can proactively seek to practice His presence throughout our day and develop an ongoing dialogue from morning to evening. In the beginning, it requires focus and determination, but soon it becomes a conversation one could not imagine living without.

Wholehearted Devotion

Mary's third encounter with Jesus was at her house before Jesus was going to be crucified. He came seeking the refuge of devoted friends, a brief respite before He entered into the most difficult days of His life. It was six days before the Passover, and Jesus knew the time had come for Him to die. Not only did He know, but He had been telling His disciples. He had told them parables of His coming death; He had told them He would suffer, He would die, He would rise again, but none of it had really made sense to them. At first, the disciples had recognized Jesus as the Messiah, a conquering hero who would finally deliver them from oppression. Slowly, this recognition of Jesus' identity had been transformed into not just the Messiah but the Son of God. But how could they now reconcile the Son of God dying? Mary had heard all of the same parables and had listened to Jesus' repeated warnings of His impending death and resurrection. Although she did not grasp exactly how it was all going to happen, her heart knew the time for all these things had drawn near.

In the place of intimacy, we are able to let go of knowing something intellectually, and we embrace another level of knowing. The experiential knowledge of knowing Jesus and being in relationship with Him brings us a new level of confidence and expectation even when intellect says it is impossible. In this depth of intimacy, we are guided by faith and our decisions are based upon this faith, a faith so certain that we can almost touch it.

Intimacy Requires Abiding

Mary only came to this level of experiential knowledge through abiding in Christ. Although for Mary it looked much different than it does for us, as Jesus was present in the flesh at that time, the words of Jesus exhorting us to abide remain foundational for growing in relationship with Him. In John 15, Jesus says that He is the Vine and the Father is the Vinedresser. This first statement helps us to understand the breadth of what He is talking about. God the Father is constantly checking the growth of the branches that are connected to the Vine.

The Father is intimately involved in our growth as His children. He is constantly checking to see if it is a dead branch with no leaves or fruit that needs to be cut off and burned or if it is a branch that is bearing fruit that needs to be pruned so it can bear more fruit. This requirement of being fruit bearers is the dividing line for the Father. We do not produce the fruit by our own effort, but it is the Spirit's work in us as we are abiding in Him. Therefore, it is not our works that produce fruitfulness, but by abiding we produce fruit. The Father is not basing our fruitfulness on ministry or success or promotion. Fruitfulness in the Kingdom of God comes as we are transformed and bear fruit that makes us look more like Jesus.

Then Jesus shares the steps to bearing fruit. First, He says, "*You were already clean because of the word which I have spoken to you*" (v.3). Here, Jesus states the beginning of fruitfulness is having relationship with Him, which we enter into through accepting the words He speaks as truth, and then those words wash us clean. This cleansing process comes by repenting of our sin and asking Jesus to wash us with His blood.

Next, Jesus unpacks abiding as the key to bearing fruit. There are two parts to this abiding. First, Jesus says, "*Abide in Me.*" We have to take deliberate steps to abide in Christ. We must make time to read His Word and pray. We need to find room in our daily schedule to come away from the busyness of life and center ourselves in His presence.

Andrew Murray wrote, "Abiding in Him is not a work that we have to do as the condition for enjoying His salvation, but a consenting to let Him do all for us, and in us, and through us." [6] It is our responsibility to choose to do certain activities that draw us into His presence, such as sitting silently before the Lord, praying while listening to worship music, or fasting. Abiding in Christ is not a passive activity. It is actively drawing near to the Lord in joyful expectation to hear His voice and respond in obedience.

As a result of our active obedience to draw near to God, Jesus says, "And I in you" (v. 4). Jesus comes and makes His dwelling inside of us. He has found a place for His Spirit to abide. We saw this same understanding of Christ dwelling in us when Paul wrote, "It is no longer I who live, but Christ lives in me" (Galatians 2:20). The life of Christ is made manifest through us. We are fully surrendered to Christ in the choices we make and the way we live our life. This is the essence of God abiding in us. He makes the fullness of Himself available to us, His power, His grace, His strength, His hope, His mercy, and His love. But this is only available to us as we first abide in Him.

Out of us abiding in Christ and Christ abiding in us, then we begin to bear fruit. There are two types of fruitfulness. The first is fruit in our inner lives. Paul refers to this as the fruit of the Spirit – love, joy, peace, patience, kindness, goodness, faithfulness, gentleness and self-control (Galatians 5:22). In the Sermon on the Mount, Jesus refers to this inner fruitfulness as developing poverty of spirit, mourning, meekness, and hungering and thirsting after righteousness. This fruit is of paramount importance because it is only as we are producing this fruit that the second type of fruit can be produced.

The second type of fruitfulness is impacting others with the gospel. We cannot expect to impact others with the gospel if the gospel is not first impacting us. As we are being changed, the life of Jesus can impact the lives of others around us. Jesus talks about this second kind of fruitfulness in the second part of the beatitudes. Jesus highlights being merciful, pure in heart, peacemakers, and persecuted for righteousness' sake. As we experience Jesus' abiding in us, we become fruitful in our relationship with others—expressing mercy; developing a purity of heart as we interact with others—not judging them or defending ourselves but loving them with a pure heart; being peacemakers both with other people as well as between people and God; and, enduring persecution. Often people are persecuted because they are impacting the lives of others. If we are not having an impact, then the enemy has no reason to persecute us. We are no threat to his kingdom if we are not advancing the Kingdom of Christ.

Both the inner fruitfulness and that which impacts others is only possible as we abide in Christ. We are wholly unable to produce more love or joy of our own power. The world creates poor imitations of the realities available in Christ's Kingdom. The world has lust, but not love. It has happiness, but not joy. To tap into the fullness of Christ, we must be connected to the Vine.

"For without Me, you can do nothing" (v. 5). This verse was a source of confusion for me when I was a young Christian. I did not understand what Jesus meant by without Him I couldn't do anything. Before I was a Christian, I did a lot of things. I see a lot of non-Christians in the world who can do lots of things. But as I studied this passage, I realized the fruitfulness Jesus refers to us in the first part of the verse is a direct correlation to the second part of the verse. Both kinds of fruitfulness mentioned above are fruit that remain for eternity. Apart from Christ, I can do nothing that impacts eternity.

Mary carried in her this abiding lifestyle. Her depth of understanding of what was happening beckoned to her spirit to pour out a lavish act of worship before Jesus died. Jesus recognized this act as more important than any of the disciples realized. She understood Jesus was dying, and because of this, Jesus said, *"Assuredly, I say to you, wherever this gospel is preached in the whole world, what this woman has done will also be told as a memorial to her"* (Matthew 26:13). Her impact is clear, not only on Jesus; but she is an illustration of what it means to possess abandoned devotion.

Intimacy Releases Understanding

Mary knew in her heart Jesus was about to die. There was no indication in the natural that this was going to happen. The Pharisees had never liked Jesus. They felt threatened by His humility and power. However, the disciples did not know the extent of their hatred. Mary had listened to what Jesus said and had pondered it in her heart, and now she sensed the time had come. Jesus had not only foretold His death but also His resurrection. His death was coming, but that meant His resurrection was also drawing near.

Intimacy releases to us understanding of our times and the confidence in faith to walk into the promises of God. As we faithfully walk with God, we go deeper into knowing God. We have passed the point of just being able to hear God's voice and receive His promises. We begin to understand God's timing of when He desires to release those promises in our lives and how we can walk them out by faith. The sons of Issachar were called the ones who understood the times and the seasons (1 Chronicles 12:32). They did not just happen upon this knowledge, nor was it a secret they discovered in a book.

Knowing the times and seasons of God's timing can only be gained by faithfully walking in intimacy with God over time. God does not entrust the ways of His Kingdom and His purposes in the Earth to the casual observer. He does not waste telling His plans to those who do not desire to engage with Him in seeing them fulfilled. God is looking for those who will not give up. He is searching for the faithful. Our commitment to go deeper still will be rewarded with the resurrection power of Jesus to see the promises of God fulfilled in His timing.

Today the Spirit is releasing understanding of His heart for His Great Commission. He is passionate for all of the ethnic people groups to be given a chance to hear the gospel in a culturally relevant way. We are given greater understanding into His heart as we draw deeper into the place of intimacy. He does not share His heart with those who are casual, but He will share with those who pursue Him. This season we are in as the body of Christ is a call to align ourselves rightly in intimacy and devotion. As we are faithful to align ourselves, God is faithful to show us His purposes in this hour of history.

Intimacy Releases Belonging

Here in this place of intimacy we find the greatest power in Christ's Kingdom. It is here in the place of intimacy where we know we belong to Him and He belongs to us. It is where we finally see ourselves as His beloved. We are accepted, just as we are. His love is not based on our actions or performance. His acceptance of us is not based on our gender or ethnicity. Christ came and died for us while we were still sinners. His love and acceptance are not earned. His love is a gift. As believers, we have all been grafted into a new family. We all are partakers of the same grace, same love, and same freedom. We all belong to Him.

Belonging to God's family is a safe place. We all come from different languages, ethnicities, family backgrounds. We all have sin, and we are all saved by grace. Sometimes, people fall into an unhealthy way of thinking concerning sin. Some think God has saved them from most of their sin, but there is some sin that cannot be forgiven. Of course, they do not say it in that way. Most often, they feel extremely guilty about something in their past. God can forgive everything else, but he cannot forgive this. Or they think that God has forgiven them, but they cannot forgive themselves. If we hold any sin back from God, whether we did it or it was done to us, we are lessening Christ's work on the cross. Either he has cleansed us from all sin or none at all. If we cannot forgive ourselves, then we are cheapening the work of Christ by saying that he did not pay enough to cover this one. Belonging to Christ's family means giving Him our whole self and allowing Him to love us completely, without holding anything back.

When we understand we are His beloved, we find a new level of freedom to be the person God has created us to be. We are not trying to do something to earn someone's approval. We find the freedom to choose God's destiny for us as well as the confidence to pursue it. We cease to care what other people think when God asks us to do something. When we know we are accepted by God, we do not look to other people to please them. Before we do something, we look to God for guidance and approval. When we know our true identity, then we act differently.

Out of the depth of Mary's devotion, she came to Jesus and anointed His feet with costly oil. She came freely with no obligation. She freely gave the costly oil to anoint His feet. She came and gave so freely because she had experienced the love of Jesus freely given to her. John writes, "We love Him because He first loved us" (1 John 4:19). Mary's lavish devotion is just a fraction of the love she had already received from Jesus. The love of Jesus inside of us does not equate deeds as the measure of our devotion. Rather, the deeds we do are an overflow of our love for Jesus. He loves our small, weak deeds of love and blesses them with the enormity of His love for us.

Intimacy Produces the Fear of the Lord

One of the key phrases in the Old Testament is "the fear of the Lord." Proverbs was written by Solomon, who is said to be the wisest king of all Israel. He petitioned the Lord to give him wisdom, and God granted him his request. The wisdom of Solomon is found in the words of Proverbs. Here, we see Solomon highlight one of the keys to having wisdom. He writes, *"The fear of the Lord is the beginning of knowledge, but fools despise wisdom and instruction"* (Proverbs 1:7). Those who are seeking to find wisdom first need the fear of the Lord.

What is the fear of the Lord?

The fear of the Lord is often misunderstood because of the word fear. Normally, we associate fear with being afraid of something bad or of a negative experience we had in the past. We imagine a drunk, alcoholic father coming home while the children cower in fear of being hit or worse. Though this may be a dramatic example, it shows us the root of what we associate with the word fear. Things that truly terrify us as adults may not be the same, but we can empathize with the fear felt by those children who were not able to stand up for themselves.

However, Father God is not one before whom we need to cower in fear. The Father is infinitely full of love, compassion and mercy. His grace extends to the worst sinner, and there is not one outside of the grasp of His forgiveness if we would only confess. He wants to move us into a right understanding of the fear of the Lord. The fear of the Lord can be better understood as a child-like dependence upon their parents.

My children wake up each morning and without hesitation ask, "What is for breakfast?" They know every day of their lives they have had breakfast provided for them, and they depend on me to have it ready or to give them options in the morning. The thought would never cross their mind that I would not have food for them. This faith and dependence are what God is desiring for us to possess. Coupled with this dependence is the understanding as an adult of what would happen if God did not provide. This understanding of our absolute dependence on God and our desperation without Him highlights the true nature of the fear of the Lord.

As we engage with God and go deeper in our relationship with Him, we desire not to do things that break our relationship, out of fear of being separated from Him. We desire not to engage in the sin life and the lusts of the flesh because we know those things bring distance between us and God. Intimacy is where we want to be as close as possible, nothing hindering our communion with Christ. Fear, then, becomes not a thing to avoid but our motivation toward right living. This fear is healthy and right. This fear cultivates within us a continuous thrust into holiness for, as the writer of Hebrews says, *"without holiness, no one will see the Lord"* (Heb. 12:14).

This essential part of the Christian life is made possible as we enter into this intimate communion with the Lord. Holiness on its own seems like a thousand rules of do's and don'ts that continually fill us with shame or pride depending upon the day or the hour. Believers who have not fully abandoned the self-life and have not embraced the repeated filling of the Spirit will be overcome by the law because they cannot see the immense grace poured out on their behalf to enable them to walk in holiness.

Our intimacy with Christ becomes the highway to holiness. As we become more intimate with Christ, we consciously choose to walk toward Christ by living a holy lifestyle. Those who are not in this place of intimate communion are easily tempted to say things they should not, do things they should not, go places they should not, look at things they should not. They sense their hearts twinge with the grief of the Holy Spirit inside of them, but they ignore the warning signs and run full throttle into those things that tear them apart from God. When we sense the nudge of the Holy Spirit, we must turn away, run away, or flee these things that will cause harm to our relationship with God. If we value our bond with God, we will choose the right response, walking in the fear of the Lord.

The Goal of Intimacy: Union With Christ

As we have progressed in this chapter from the beginning stages of intimacy, we have looked at focusing our energy on saying "yes" to Him when we have the opportunity to enter into His presence; deliberately choosing to abide in Him; building the deeper relationship of a willingness to sacrifice because of the reality of the knowledge of the fullness of Christ living inside of us; and, out of that reality, choosing to walk in holiness because of our fear of the Lord. This has all been leading us and preparing us for the marriage supper of the Lamb, where the Bride of Christ will be fully joined to Christ. This is a mystical union God has created for us as believers. This union has been in His plan since the beginning of time, and we partake of this mystical union gradually over time until on that Day when the fullness of this union comes to pass.

In the beginning, God created man, but God saw in man a need for communion and intimacy. God made man and gave to him the responsibility of keeping the garden and tending to the animals He had made. God saw Adam was alone without a mate of his own. In order to rectify this, God could have made Eve out of the dust just as He had created Adam. But God chose to cause Adam to fall asleep in order for God to take out ribs and make Eve (Gen. 2:8-25). God's chosen path, bringing out of Adam one who was like him and a suitable helper to him, sheds new light on our own union with Christ.

God's purposed design in creation is similar to what we experience in our walk with Christ. Paul brings this to light, *"For the husband is the head of the wife, as also Christ is the head of the church. ... Husbands, love your wives, just as Christ also loved the church and gave Himself for her"* (Ephesians 5:23,25). God intended for us to see in creation a model not only for human marriage but also for the marriage between Jesus and the church. God has designed us to walk in the same intimacy we find in marriage to Him as His Bride. In the same way we share our lives with our spouse in communication, in physical, emotional, and spiritual intimacy, and in time spent together, Christ wants us to have this same intimacy with Him.

While marriage is a helpful picture to begin to imagine the depth of intimacy Christ desires to have with us, it is still incomplete. God desires for us the intimacy found in marriage and more. He is not satisfied for us to go places with Him or do things with Him. God seeks to build the very character of God inside of us when Paul writes, *"Christ also loved the church and gave Himself for her so that He might sanctify and cleanse her with the washing of the water by the word"* (Ephesians 5:25-26). Here, we see Paul highlight the conditional nature of the church's existence. Only through Christ's death and resurrection was the church born. Just as Eve came from Adam, so too the church is born through Christ's death and resurrection. The church is then enabled to grow through the reading of God's Word because Christ has made this possible through His death and resurrection.

This new union with Christ is the goal of our intimacy with Him. We desire to have His abiding presence in us as we abide in Him. We want to have the mind of Christ inside of us to make the right decisions, choosing what Christ would. The fullness of God inside of us comes with His emotions, too: *"joy inexpressible and full of glory"* as Peter writes or the *"fullness of joy"* as David writes in the Psalms (1 Peter 1:8; Psalm 16:11). The union Christ intends for us to walk in is a complete submission to the Holy Spirit. We do not get to hold back some parts for ourselves, such as our emotions or some events of our past. Union is not complete until we are fully surrendered.

This union happens through two ways. The first is the Bride making herself ready (Revelation 19:7). This part of making ourselves ready is through what we have already talked about in living a holy lifestyle. Our choices have a significant impact on how ready we are to be united with Christ. The choice of surrender is not an easy one, but it is necessary for entering into the fullness of God's destiny for us. We must continually prioritize His character being formed in us, and following His ways and not our own.

Secondly, we see the Bride being clothed in fine linen and apparel. This is the work of the Father in our lives. God comes and clothes us with the robes of righteousness purchased by the blood of His Son. He exchanges the heavy yoke of shame and pleasing other people with humility and meekness. These are gifts He bestows upon us that we cannot earn or make ourselves. It is His work of grace in our lives. His responsibility is to produce fruit in our lives, while our job is to remain and abide in Him in order for Him to produce this fruit. Although this mystical union we experience here on Earth is designed to affect every part of us, we will experience yet another dimension of this union when we stand face to face with our Bridegroom on that glorious day of the wedding feast.

Contemplation:

As you reflect on your intimacy with Christ, do you see yourself growing in love and devotion? Looking back at the pictures of Mary's devotion, are you also deliberately trying to be single-minded in following Christ? Are you focused on building relationship with the Lord? Are you working on growing in confidence, in understanding of God's seasons, and in the abiding that produces fruitfulness?

No matter where you are, none of us has arrived at the greatest level of intimacy available to us. Jesus is constantly offering more of Himself to us, if we would but ask. I have never read of anyone who has said, "I know everything about God." But rather, it is the opposite: The more we grow in God, the more we realize how much more of God is available to us. We can never fully know the bounds of His love, mercy, grace and power.

The key to growing is finding the time to wait at His feet and being hungry for Him to meet with us. Making the time to sit in His presence. You cannot hurry the process. You cannot accomplish in five minutes what God will do in an hour. We have to be focused and determined to not relent. We must purposefully pursue Him and His presence in our lives.

1. We cannot take someone else further than what we have experienced ourselves. Can you identify one theme the Lord is highlighting to you where you want to go deeper? Intimacy is a multifaceted dynamic of the Spirit, and you can't work on everything at the same time. The key is to work in step with the Spirit. Thank the Lord for the measure of this theme you already understand and ask Him to deepen your understanding and revelation.

2. What is something the Lord is highlighting for you to share with someone else? As you were reading, the Holy Spirit prompted you with stories of your own. Take your own experience of hearing God's voice or of an intimate time in prayer and share it with someone to encourage them in their walk with the Lord. We are all called to be

disciples, which means we need more mature Christians speaking into our lives as well as finding those younger in the faith whom we can exhort and encourage. Use your voice today to call others deeper.

Prayer:

Lord, I want more of You. I have been content in my heart with the understanding that I have right now, but I want a greater revelation. Make me hungry for more. I want to hear Your voice more clearly and accomplish those things that are on Your heart. Take me deeper in the place of abiding in order to bear more fruit for your Kingdom and glory. Cause me to walk in holiness before You for Your fullness to be in me. In Jesus' name I pray, AMEN.

4

Understanding God's Character

Cultivating a lifestyle of abandoned devotion means we are on a journey of deep calling unto deep. As we go deeper in God, we are stirred with a passion to go deeper still. We will never come to the end of knowing everything about God, but we can know more than we know right now. Throughout this journey of brokenness and intimacy, the Lord is revealing more of Himself to us. To grow more in our relationship with God, we need to actively pursue knowing more of His character and His ways.

The more time we spend with God, the more we understand His character and His ways. Just like in a marriage, someone newly married does not know how their spouse will react in certain circumstances because they have not spent much time together. Conversely, a couple who has been married for 50 years is intimately acquainted with the behaviors of their spouse. This couple knows their routine throughout the day, and it is likely they would be able to predict one another's decisions and reactions.

Fortunately for us, we do not have to rely solely upon our own experience with God, but we can study the lives of others in the Bible.

We can see how God revealed Himself to them, how they walked with God, how God reacted in different circumstances. This is an amazing treasure trove of many different insights into God's character and His ways of interacting and dealing with us. As we read the Word of God, we need to be purposeful in asking God to teach us what we can understand about His character and His ways. Similarly, when we go through circumstances in our lives, every situation—whether good or bad—is an opportunity for us to learn more about God and His ways. It is easier to see God's grace and love when things are going well in our lives. But the real challenge is to learn these deep lessons about God's character and His ways as we go through difficult circumstances in our lives.

As we study the Bible, we can get snapshots of different facets of God's character. The Lord is multi-faceted and has so many wonderful qualities and attributes that I could not presume to create an exhaustive list. However, one description of God is used by God Himself. It is also used throughout the whole of the Old Testament Pentateuch, Writings, Prophets, and Historical books. In Exodus 34:6-7, the Lord gives this description of Himself:

> "And the Lord passed before him and proclaimed, 'The Lord,
> the Lord God merciful and gracious, longsuffering, and
> abounding in lovingkindness, keeping mercy for thousands,
> forgiving iniquity and transgression and sin, by no means
> clearing the guilty, visiting the iniquity of the fathers upon the
> children and the children's children to the third and the fourth
> generation'" (Exodus 34:6-7).

This stunning self-portrait of God is also found in Numbers 14:18, Nehemiah 9:17, 2 Samuel 12:22, Joel 2:13, Jonah 4:2, Psalms 86:5, 15 and 103:8-10. Not only is this how God speaks of Himself, but this is also how He revealed Himself to His people throughout many generations. These four characteristics are the capstone of God's character: merciful or compassionate; gracious; longsuffering or slow to anger; and full of lovingkindness. While this list is not exhaustive of the many wonderful characteristics of God, these give a picture of the Lord's character and the ways He deals with us. We want to look at each of these four characteristics in order to understand why God highlighted just these four out of the many He could have emphasized such as just, holy and righteous.

Compassion and Mercy

God the Father begins with this revelation because it is only through His compassion and mercy that we are able to come into His presence. Compassion and mercy are qualities of God referring to taking pity on a person or people who are suffering. Throughout the Scriptures, the image of the Father taking pity on His children and rescuing them, delivering them, feeding them, and caring for them is a faithful portrait of God's mercy and compassion at work.

Not only does Moses understand himself, who as a baby was rescued by Pharaoh's daughter, as a recipient of this mercy, but he also sees the Israelites as recipients of God's mercy. As they were delivered from Egypt, God poured out His mercy to save them from their suffering in Egypt. While they were in the wilderness, God had compassion on them when they had no water and brought forth water from a rock. When they were hungry and did not have enough food, God had mercy on them and fed them with manna from heaven every morning for 40 years.

These pictures of God's compassionate nature are given a new dimension as Christ comes to earth. No longer is it God in heaven having mercy and compassion, but it is Jesus in the flesh demonstrating the ways of God for all to see. Jesus had gone to a deserted place to pray, but the people desperate for His presence followed Him to that place. They had brought all the sick people they knew, and Jesus *"saw a great multitude, and He was moved with compassion for them, and healed their sick"* (Matthew 14:14). He didn't just say what a sorry and misfortunate group of people they were and then move on. He looked into their eyes, and His heart was touched by their pain and suffering.

This is the God we serve. One who is moved by our pain and suffering. With the same compassion He had for this great multitude, He wants to bring healing and wholeness as He did with the two blind men who received their sight (Matthew 20:34); He wants to feed those who are hungry like the 4,000 who continued being with Jesus for three straight days and had no food left (Matthew 15:32); He wants to deliver those who are oppressed in bondage like the boy with a mute spirit who had seizures (Mark 9:22); and He wants to teach those who lack the understanding of His ways like the multitude who were like sheep with no shepherd and He began to teach them (Mark 6:34). God's compassion runs deep, and we will never exhaust it.

Yet, it is not enough for Jesus to possess this compassion and mercy; He calls us to be like Himself and possess it ourselves. Jesus was being tested by a lawyer about how to inherit eternal life. The lawyer responded to Jesus that the two greatest commandments are to love God and love your neighbor as yourself. But the lawyer, trying to understand the bounds of who we are required to love, asked Jesus which people he has to love. Jesus responded by telling him the parable of the Good Samaritan. This Samaritan man was looked down upon because of his ethnicity. Having no religious training or profession of serving, he simply acted with mercy toward one who was suffering. Jesus exhorts this Jewish lawyer to go and be like this Samaritan, showing compassion and mercy to others.

Jesus also highlights this quality in the Sermon on the Mount. In the fifth beatitude, Jesus says, *"Blessed are the merciful for they shall obtain mercy"* (Matthew 5:7). God is the one who has complete and perfect compassion and mercy, but it is not enough for only Himself to have it. He wants His children to possess His same characteristics. We are called to have this same mercy as we interact with others, taking pity on them in their suffering because Jesus has done the same for us. We have freely received the Lord's mercy time and again, and we must choose to enter into His life and be a conduit of His life to others.

Gracious

Grace is God's undeserved favor toward humanity. In the Old Testament, we see the grace of God explained as finding "favor in the eyes of the Lord." Many people throughout the Old Testament carry this description, and it is often spoken in contrast to those who have not found favor but rather judgment for their wickedness. The term grace is pervasive in its use in the New Testament. From the gospels to the epistles, we see this term used specifically as a divine characteristic. Professor Andrew H. Trotter Jr. writes of the term grace, "Again, these phrases often seem to be linked with the power of God to create spiritual life and sustain Christians. This grace is, as in the Old Testament passages, an unmerited favor, but now a new aspect of power in the Spirit has been added to it." [7] This added dimension to the concept of grace expands our understanding of God's grace in our lives from merely His unmerited favor to an empowering through His Spirit for life and ministry.

Here in this passage in Exodus, Moses has entered the holy place of God's presence, speaking to God almost as if they were face-to-face. This intimacy in Moses' relationship with God is only possible because of God's grace. God's grace was even extended to Moses in a way no one on Earth has ever experienced again—when Moses asked to behold His glory. No one could see God and live, so the Lord let Moses behold the back of His glory so he would not die. Even when God answered and revealed Himself, which was unmerited favor, He still was careful to only let Moses see what would not kill him. Moses did not understand the full measure of what he was asking. But God did. In His grace, He did not grant Moses something that would have harmed him.

Even though Moses is referred to as the humblest man on Earth at that time (Numbers 12:3), he was still a sinner, and a sinner cannot come into God's presence apart from God's enabling grace being poured out. Let us not forget that Moses had murdered a man in cold blood, and then he buried the body in the sand to cover up his crime. Moses understood he did not deserve God's grace. Our past sins do not have to determine our present experience of God. Our repentance makes us new, and God's empowering grace enables us to walk not according to the old man but as His new creation.

In the same manner, Paul writes in Romans, *"But God demonstrates His own love toward us, in that while we were still sinners, Christ died for us. ... But the free gift is not like the offense [or sin]. For if by the one man's [Adam] offense [or sin] many died, much more the grace of God and the gift by the grace of the one Man, Jesus Christ, abounded to many"* (Romans 6:8,15). While we had nothing to offer God, God came and gave us a free gift of His grace, His only begotten Son. We had done nothing to earn it; we had no power to attain it ourselves. It is only by His grace that we have been given the gift of salvation.

It is easy to limit the gift of God's grace to salvation alone. However, His grace goes far beyond this one act of saving us through the death and resurrection of Christ. Peter was one who could testify of Jesus' grace going far beyond the cross. Peter had denied Jesus three times, and then he looked into the eyes of Jesus and glimpsed His perfect love and was cut to the heart. After Jesus' resurrection, Peter experienced the power of forgiveness and the power of restoration. Peter thought his calling to be "the rock" had been lost, and that he was useless in Christ's Kingdom. However, Jesus showed Peter the depths of His grace to not only restore him in relationship but also enable to do the ministry of feeding Christ's sheep (John 21:15-19). Later in Peter's life, he testified to the empowering grace of God upon his life when he wrote his epistles. He realized God's grace releases the Lord's power and authority in our lives for all we need in life and ministry (2 Peter 1:2-3).

God's grace is not only related to our salvation, but it is by His grace we are empowered to walk in His authority and perform the same miracles Jesus did and more. His grace enables us to become those who possess the power of Christ here in our spheres of influence. As Jesus was sending out the 12 disciples into ministry, Jesus spoke to them, *"Heal the sick, cleanse the lepers, raise the dead, cast out demons.*

Freely you have received, freely give" (Matthew 10:8). This powerful statement exemplifies the free enabling grace we have been given to use the authority and power Christ has given us to extend the same grace to others. We have been given free grace to freely give away and be a conduit of Christ's grace to others. The grace of God should be a mark of every true believer, causing us to walk in the fullness of God's calling.

Longsuffering

In some translations, this word longsuffering can be translated as "slow to anger." The picture of God as one who is longsuffering is sometimes lost on those who read the Old Testament. They see only a picture of God as a God of wrath who is continually wiping out people who disobey or do not follow His ways. God's nature of being longsuffering helps us to understand the constant tension of His judgment and mercy. For God to be longsuffering means He actually will suffer a long time, hoping and interceding that we might repent so He can release mercy instead of judgment.

Whether we speak of God's judgment or His mercy, God never relinquishes His justice. Oftentimes, people see God's wrath as being capricious. They ask questions such as, "Why did God need to kill these people?" or "Why were those people saved?" God's justice requires sin be dealt with either through repentance, which enables God to release mercy, or a lack of repentance, which requires God's judgment. In either case, God is completely just because God's holiness cannot tolerate sin. It must be dealt with.

God is not a God who is continually angry, looking to see who He can crush next. He is loving and merciful, and He is eager to pour out His mercy if we will only repent. This is the description He gives of Himself. He is desiring relationship, but He cannot be close to those who are full of sin. He will go to great lengths and suffer long in order to draw His people back to Himself. He beckons to them, woos them, stirs them, all in hopes they will repent.

We see this so clearly in the Old Testament during the times of the judges. The people would follow hard after Him and then slowly begin to sink into compromise, worshipping other gods. He sent them into captivity, hoping the dire circumstances would lead them back to Him. He sent them judges to preach the message of repentance and show them the way back to God. Then, as soon as the judge had died, they would start the cycle all over again. The Father is not harsh, looking to destroy them. The Father is longsuffering and patient with us in our weakness to draw us back to Himself.

In the New Testament, we see Christ as the one who is slow to anger and always desiring mercy. In the story of the woman caught in adultery, Jesus illustrates what it looks like to be longsuffering and highlights that His nature desires mercy. Here, the Pharisees thought they had caught Jesus in another trap. This woman had been caught in the act of adultery and according to the law should be stoned. But Jesus, not rushing to judgment but reaching for mercy, knelt down and began to write in the sand. While we do not know what He wrote, it is clear the Pharisees, who stood with stones raised ready to punish her, slowly began to leave. Then Jesus, who had every right to condemn her because He Himself was perfectly sinless, said to the woman to go and change the way she had been living and sin no more. God had the power to condemn, but He chose mercy instead.

God is so patient with us, desiring us to turn to Him, and rend our hearts and not our clothes. He does not want outward acts of humiliation, but instead He wants us to possess hearts that quickly repent. David possessed this attitude toward God. When David was confronted with his sin, he quickly repented and embraced the forgiveness of God. This is why David is called "a man after God's own heart" (1 Samuel 13:14). David understood sin separates us from God, but our repentance brings us back into fellowship with Him.

We can choose to walk in bitterness and unforgiveness, compromise and outright sin, or we can choose to surrender our hearts to the Lord and turn to Him in repentance. The faster we turn to Him, the easier it is to step back into the place of intimacy in our relationship with Him. Unconfessed sin, bitterness and unforgiveness will create a wall of division between us and God. God draws back from us because we have not repented, then we draw back from God because we do not sense His nearness any longer. God will suffer long with us and continue to try and draw us back to Himself. Sometimes, His kindness allows us to come to the end of ourselves to helps us realize our desperate state without Him. Though we can easily find ourselves far from God, the road back to Him is just as easy, returning to our first love in repentance.

God calls us to possess this same quality of longsuffering. As we look at the fruit of the Spirit, we see this same quality. The fruit of the Spirit is not something we can work at or try to earn. The fruit of the Spirit is fruit born from Christ living inside of us and producing His nature within us. Human nature does not possess this quality naturally. The only way to see longsuffering produced in our lives is for us to receive it from the Holy Spirit. We can ask the Lord to increase our capacity for longsuffering, just as we can with the other fruit of the Spirit, but we cannot produce these in and of ourselves.

Paul exhorts us in Ephesians 4:2, *"I, therefore, the prisoner of the Lord, beseech you to walk worthy of the calling with which you were called, with all lowliness and gentleness, with longsuffering, bearing with one another in love."* And again, Paul writes in Colossians 3:12, *"Therefore as the elect of God, holy and beloved, put on tender mercies [compassion], kindness, humility, meekness, longsuffering."* These exhortations from Paul call us to be clothed in this same characteristic of God the Father. Notice Paul writes, we are called to "put on" these qualities. It is not something we muster up in our flesh. These are gifts we receive from God and in which we clothe ourselves. We are supposed to ask God to clothe us in these characteristics; we need to ask Him to fill us with the fruit of the Spirit. We can choose to walk according to the Spirit and put away the temptations of the flesh.

Lovingkindness

This word "lovingkindness" is very rich in meaning. Though some translations choose to simplify the meaning to simply "love" or "mercy," the fullness of the word in the Hebrew language goes far beyond this. It is easy to romanticize love or to make it all about us, but this lovingkindness of God goes to the depths of who He is. His covenant and His lovingkindness are often coupled together in the Old Testament, linking the promise-keeping loyalty of God with His steadfast love for His children. God's steadfast love does not mean an easy life for His children. He often allows circumstances and suffering to test and grow our faith, but He does this out of love for us. He does not want us to stay where we are. He desires for us to grow and mature in His likeness.

God's lovingkindness is often linked to His compassion and mercy. This lovingkindness is an expression of God's strength to deliver us. In our covenantal relationship, God is the stronger of the two parties who can offer us protection and deliverance in our times of need. Because of His great love, He releases mercy to us. Romans 6:8 says, *"But God demonstrates His own love toward us, in that while we were still sinners, Christ died for us."* God demonstrated His love to rescue us from our sin by sending His own Son to die upon the cross. It was this great act of love where God gave us His Son because it was something that we could not do ourselves. We were reliant on His strength and power. We were completely dependent upon His steadfast love to deliver us out of darkness and bring us into the Kingdom of His Son, the Kingdom of Light.

God shows the immensity of His own love by describing it as His own "abundant lovingkindness." This picture of God's love is not like a glass of water which as soon as we drink it is gone. God's love is a huge reservoir that we can never exhaust; nor even come to fully understand the bounds of His great love. Paul prays for us to be able to experientially comprehend the width, length, depth and height of God's love, which is so much more than just knowledge we gain from a book (Ephesians 3:18-19).

Ezekiel had a vision of the temple with a sacred river flowing out from under it. (Ezekiel 47:1-5) This river has strong similarities to other passages of Scripture in Joel 3:18, Zechariah 14:8 and Revelation 22:1. While this river may give us a glimpse into what the New Jerusalem will be like, we can also take lessons from this picture as it relates to God's love. In Ezekiel's vision, he began on the edge of the water and first moved until the water covered his ankles. Then, he moved until the water covered his knees. Next, the water covered up to his waist. Finally, going out further, he found the water so deep he could not cross but had to swim.

As we talk about journeying with God, I think this picture is an accurate description of us walking into and experiencing the love of God. This picture gives us several different perspectives in relation to the love of God. There are some people who stand on the very edge of the water and do not want to get their feet wet because the river of God's love seems scary because it is so immense. Unable to say "yes" to something they cannot fully comprehend, they remain skeptics who sit on the river's edge.

The second group is those who have said "yes" to wanting to experience the love of God. They have entered in only up to their ankles. Some of these who are ankle deep are there because the love of God is new to them, and they are only just beginning their journey with God. Still, there are others ankle deep who are content to stay where they are in control of their journey. It is nice to get their feet wet, being refreshed by God's love here and there. But they have no desire to move into the deeper waters of God's love to more fully experience the width, length, depth and height of God's love.

The third group are those who are in up to their knees. These people have surrendered more of their own mobility to God's love. They experience more of God's blessings, and yet some of these choose to remain here where they can still move according to their own will. They feel the resistance of the Spirit asking them to surrender more, but they are determined to do it in their own strength. Often, for these people, they will either fall back or choose to go further in surrender.

The fourth group is those who have ventured as far as one can in their own strength. Some of these people are in the process of moving toward the depths of God's love and are ready to receive God's fullness inside of them. Others are using all of their physical strength to accomplish God's purpose in their lives, without fully surrendering to His love. This is often where people become burned out. They know enough about God and His plans that they become so excited and dive into ministry. But a lack of surrender to let the ministry flow out of their relationship with God and a driven desire to make the vision come to pass leaves them burned out, hurting those around them they love the most, and causing physical, emotional and spiritual pain.

The final group is those who have surrendered to God's love completely. They do not withhold any area of their lives, and they experience the full measure of Christ living inside of them. This experience of God's love allows us to surrender to the Holy Spirit in the river and move with the current. We are moved to do the things the Spirit is highlighting to us. This does not mean there are no challenges or spiritual attacks to those living in the place of full surrender. But it does mean they have the fullness of God inside of them to overcome those challenges and difficulties, rather than being overcome.

Being at the beach, I have seen countless people stand in the water and watch the waves crash over them. I have done it myself even, but it is exhausting to stay where I have to fight against the waves to stand up. Those who stay in the water a long time go beyond the place where one can only stand. They go out into the deep where waves are not crashing down upon them, but they are floating above the waves. They feel the waves flow underneath them, but they are not overcome by them. Similarly in our spiritual lives, when we surrender to the depths of God's love, we actually experience His Spirit buoying us up.

God's love is strong and steadfast and enables us to overcome the waves. God's love is unending, an inexhaustible supply. No matter what we have done in the past, He still has more love to bring us back to Himself. God's love is sweet, gentle and tender. He does not come in and overwhelm us, but He quietly waits for us to draw nearer to Him and seek His face. God is love, and nothing we do can separate us from God's love unless we choose to walk away. (Rom. 8:38-39)

Contemplation:

As we reflect on God's character and His ways of drawing us to Himself, and His desire to make us more like Himself, what are some of the areas where you need to grow? What is the Spirit saying He wants to speak to you today?

1. What are some of the new insights you have gleaned about God? What are some of these characteristics the Lord is wanting to grow in you? We cannot just build up a heap of knowledge about God, which is what the Pharisees did. We have to actually have the truth living inside of us. We need our understanding of who God is to change the way we look at events in our lives. It can no longer be truth that is external to us, but it must shape our everyday experience of God and our life in Him.

2. What new insight about God's character can you share with someone today? Every day, we should be growing in our understanding of God. The vast ocean of God cannot be comprehended in one lifetime. Learn from others and ask them what they are learning about God's character and ways.

Prayer:

Lord, I do not just want to know more about You intellectually. I want to experience Your character and Your ways and then make these realities in my life. Give me eyes to see who You are, ears to hear how You interact with Your people, and a heart to understand what You are saying. Holy Spirit, I cannot do this without Your help. Birth in me the character and ways of God so that I can have the fullness of Christ inside of me. In Jesus' name, AMEN.

5

Complete Obedience
Walking Out Our Love

Throughout the journey in our walk with God, God requires one important thing, our complete obedience. Whether it is in the beginning of our journey through the wilderness of brokenness, and we sense God asking us to forgive someone who hurt us when we were very young, we have to give God our complete obedience. At times in the place of intimacy with God, we see some of our habits are not pleasing to the Lord, and He asks us to stop doing them. We have to give God our complete obedience. During our walk, we are constantly learning more about the character of God, and God asks us to choose meekness rather than defend ourselves when someone attacks us. We have to give God our complete obedience.

Although it is easy to fall into the trap of busyness and forget to do something, or in trying to stop doing something we fail and give up trying because it is just too hard, or the attack was so personal we just had to defend our honor, we will always find a way to excuse our disobedience. But it is our disobedience that will hinder our growth. This does not mean we only get one chance, but it does mean we commit ourselves to grow and try again. We cannot just give up. As we talked about in the previous chapter, God is gracious to forgive us and set us back on track. We just have to run back to Him again and set our hearts to obey.

The Importance of Obedience

In the last chapter, we talked about God's love as one of His chief characteristics and how we must possess that same love inside of us. As God gives us His love, it is with that same love we love Him back. In Matthew 22, the Pharisees were trying to test Jesus and asked Him what is the greatest commandment. Jesus replies,

> "You shall love the LORD your God with all your heart, with all your soul, and with all your mind. This is the first and greatest commandment. And the second is like it, 'You shall love your neighbor as yourself'" (Matthew 22:37-39).

This is the call upon our lives to love Jesus more, with our whole being. But this is often misinterpreted as meaning that the way to love God is to love other people. While it is good to love other people, this is not the highest priority in how to love God. Jesus Himself tells us how we are to show our love for Him.

In John 14, Jesus unfolds this theme of love being shown through obedience. Jesus begins by saying, "If you love me, keep My commandments" (John 14:15). Then He repeats this theme again in verse 21, "He who has My commandments and keeps them, it is he who loves Me." And once again He emphasizes in verse 23, "If anyone loves Me, he will keep My word; and My father will love him." Finally, in verse 24, He highlights the negative, "He who does not love Me does not keep My words." Jesus repeats the same theme four times in the space of nine verses. This clear repetition gives us clarity of what our love should look like. Our obedience expresses our love to God.

In essence, Jesus is saying His true disciples will be known by their obedience. James says the same thing slightly differently, "But be doers of the word and not hearers only." We cannot merely hear the Scriptures and expect to be called a Christian. Christians are those who do what they read and hear. Christians who love other people but are not being obedient to what God is asking them to do are not really loving God. However, as we love God and walk in obedience, the natural overflow of this will be loving other people.

This theme of obedience as the centerpiece of true discipleship is found throughout the Bible. In Deuteronomy, Moses goes over all of the things he had told the people and reminded them of the things God had done in their midst. In case some of his listeners needed the CliffsNotes version, Moses writes,

> *"And now, Israel, what does the LORD your God require of you, but to fear the LORD your God, to walk in all His ways and to love Him, to serve the LORD your God with all your heart and with all your soul, and to keep the commandments of the LORD and His statutes which I command you today for your good?"* (Deuteronomy 10:12-13).

This encapsulates the fullness of what God is asking of His people in their relationship with Him. Moses follows this list of expectations with what should happen next. Moses writes, *"Therefore you shall love the LORD your God, and keep His charge, His statutes, His judgments, and His commandments always"* (Deuteronomy 11:1). Because we are in relationship with the living God, He has expectations, and we meet these expectations by loving Him through our obedience.

Every day, God gives us many opportunities to choose obedience. As we grow in hearing God's voice and experiencing new facets of God's nature in us, God requires us to keep responding. We hear God's voice ask us to write a note to a friend. We must make a deliberate choice to take time out of our busy day and do the thing God is asking of us. God is challenging our responses and asking us to make the hard choices to say "yes" to Him and "no" to the plethora of other demands for our attention.

Leaders Called to a Higher Standard

For those people in ministry leadership, there is a greater level of accountability. Because people are looking to leaders for spiritual advice, our disobedience is put on display for everyone to see and sets a bad example. Therefore, the consequences are much more serious. Leaders must be very careful to quickly obey whatever the Lord is asking. The faster we obey, the easier it is. There is less time to create excuses, forget or procrastinate.

The Life of Saul

In 1 Samuel, we read the story of Saul, a king who fit the expectations of the people in his outward characteristics. God desired the people to see Him as their King, but the lack of leadership in Israel had created a tendency for them to wander from their covenant relationship with Yahweh. Reluctantly, God gave them a king to rule over them. He selected Saul, from the tribe of Benjamin, who was tall and looked like a king on the outside, what the people expected of a king.

However, Saul quickly found himself in trouble as king over Israel. After reigning only two years in this newly created position, he started a war with the Philistines, sending his son Jonathan to attack a stronghold of the Philistines in Geba. This attack incited the Philistines, and they rallied 30,000 chariots and 6,000 horsemen plus a great multitude of infantry against Saul's paltry army of 3,000 men. Samuel had set the time for the burnt offering and sacrifice for seven days after they arrived at the camp. These seven days of waiting began to rattle the men, and slowly they began to leave until only 600 remained.

Saul's sudden thrust into leadership had left him unprepared for the tests and trials of leading such a large group of people. Had he looked to the Lord in his inexperience, the Lord would have supplied all that he needed. But instead, Saul easily fell into the trap of wanting to please the people so they would not scatter and leave. Thinking his act was speeding up the obedience required before going to war, he decided to just offer the burnt offering himself, rather than waiting for

Samuel as he was supposed to do. However, Samuel arrived as soon as he had finished. Appalled at Saul's actions, Samuel declared that Saul's disobedience had cost him his throne being established forever.

Saul could have changed at this point and repented, recovering at least his throne for the present, but he did not repent. He did not choose to admit his mistakes and draw upon God's mercy. Saul had not walked intimately with the Lord and did not know God's character or His ways. He was unable to discern the necessary steps to seeing restoration. Instead, Saul continued to think he knew best and that his version of obedience was enough.

Samuel went to Saul to tell him to go to war with the Amalekites because of their mistreatment of Israel as they came out of Egypt. Samuel clearly told Saul what he was expected to do: *"Now go and attack Amalek, and utterly destroy all that they have, and do not spare them. But kill both man and woman, infant and nursing child, ox and sheep, camel and donkey"* (1 Samuel 15:3). Saul listened to Samuel's words and then headed off to war with 200,000 soldiers and 10,000 men from Judah. They demolished the Amalekites, and in victory they returned. *"But Saul and the people spared Agag [the king of the Amalekites] and the best of the sheep, the oxen, the fatlings, the lambs, and all that was good, and were unwilling to utterly destroy them"* (v.9).

Saul had moved from trying to speed up the ritual of the burnt offering to totally disregarding the commandment of the Lord and being completely unwilling to do as he was told. He had not learned from his previous mistake. Samuel came to him after the battle and showed him his lack of obedience. In Saul's twisted way of thinking, he had obeyed, but anything less than full obedience is sin. Though Saul said the words of repentance, Samuel knew that his heart was only wanting to make things look good before the people. Saul's heart had not really changed; he was still only concerned about pleasing people. Saul's lack of regard for God's ways cost him his kingdom. In desperation, Saul grasped for Samuel's robe trying to force him to stay, but it was only a further symbolic pronouncement that the kingdom of Israel had been torn from him that very day.

This severe discipline of the Lord may seem harsh or excessive for what were seemingly small mistakes in following God, but God does not just look at the mistake, He looks at the heart. Saul's heart was bent on pleasing people and not committed to following God. As the leader of Israel, people would follow and imitate what they saw in the leadership of the people. The Lord could not allow such an example of disobedience remain for others to follow. The Lord saw that Saul would not change, and He would need to raise up a new king who would follow in God's ways.

The Life of Moses

Another example of the consequences of our disobedience is in the life of Moses. Moses, a giant in the faith who walked with God so closely his face glowed with the glory of God, had his own struggle with carefully following all of God's instructions. In this world where it is easy to cut corners, we would probably give Moses a passing grade for his obedience to God. But alas, God did not look so kindly upon Moses' compromise before the Israelites. In Numbers 20, we read the account of the Israelites in the Wilderness of Zin in the place called Kadesh. Once again, the people are stirred up to complain against Aaron and Moses because there is no water. Previously, when the people complained about not having water, Moses prayed and struck the rock with his staff, resulting in water pouring forth. This time, however, Moses prayed and God asked him to speak to the rock, but instead Moses struck the rock again. Even though Moses did not completely obey, water still poured forth from the rock.

But God rebuked Moses for not completely following the instructions he was given. As a consequence, Moses was not permitted to go into the Promised Land. While we may think this was not such a big deal, we must remember the Promised Land is the only hope Moses had of getting out of the wilderness with the Israelites. He had looked forward to seeing the Promised Land for 40 long years, 40 years of listening to complaints, 40 years of people asking him when they would finally arrive at their destination. Now, at the moment when they were almost there, the one thing he had been longing for was taken away. Although God had to punish Moses' sin, the Lord had mercy on him and let him gaze upon the Promised Land from Mount Nebo, where he died. Moses' sin cost him entering his land of inheritance.

As leaders, we are called to a higher level of accountability in our obedience to God. Our compromise is put on display for everyone to see. We cannot expect God to let us off the hook for leading His sheep astray. Rather, we are challenged to a higher standard of righteousness and obedience in our calling and leadership. Our obedience brings glory to God and shows that God is in charge and not us. We will not just do things the way they have always been done, but we will ask God and follow his leading and guidance in the process.

The Life of David

David is an example of one who lived his life in complete obedience to God. Obviously, David has his share of sin written on the pages of history, just as we all do. However, it is what we do with our sin that matters. David did not revel in his sin. He was faithful to repent every time, turn from his sin, and change his ways.

David's story of obedience is not limited to successes or failures. His obedience comes from a heart that is hidden in God. He did not cry out for attention. He did not go looking for Samuel to make him king. He was content with being obedient to God in every moment and being found faithful and obedient in the small things. Early in his life, David was charged with taking care of the sheep. He had to protect them against lions and bears, and he faithfully did this even when no one else observed his actions. Alone in the field, he chose not to please people or save his own life but rather to faithfully fulfill his duty to protect the sheep.

David was anointed king at the age of about 15, but he would not come into the first fruits of his reign over one of tribes of Israel for seven and a half years, and then he would wait another seven and a half years until he received the fullness of the kingship promised 15 years earlier.

As we wait upon God and His timing, we will receive His promises, but we have to remain obedient.

David was tested many times as he ran for his life when Saul was trying to kill him. David had several opportunities to kill Saul in order to become king, but he would not rush God's timing. He was obedient to stay in the place God had for him. Even when Saul died, David did not rush to Gilgal to become the king of Israel. But rather he asked the Lord, *"Should I go to the any of the cities in Judah?"* Judah was his own tribe, but he did not presume the Lord would call him to a place where he would find friends and family. When the Lord said yes, he was mindful to ask which one and not just go to Bethlehem, where he was born. His patient obedience was characteristic of David throughout his life.

The Life of Jesus

The ultimate example of obedience is found in the life of Jesus. His obedience throughout His life is total and complete. From the beginning of His incarnation, He willingly limited His divine nature to take on human likeness in order for us to be restored to relationship with the Father. *"Jesus told the people, 'I tell you for certain that the Son cannot do anything on His own. He can do only what He sees the Father doing, and He does exactly what He sees the Father do'"* (John 5:19, CEV). Jesus was consistently obedient throughout His life to only do what He saw the Father doing. He did not try to make it up as He went along. He did not try to deviate from the divine plan.

Jesus lived in the place of obedience. When He would go away to pray to the Father, He did not have to begin His prayer by asking for forgiveness for all of the wrong things He had done. He did not need to repent for His sins. His prayer was instant communication through the Holy Spirit to the Father. We can learn not only from Christ's death and resurrection, but also through the manner in which He lived His life in complete obedience to the Father.

Some would say Jesus had it easy because all He did was walk around healing people, casting out demons, and preaching the good news. Who wouldn't want to spend their life making a vast impact for God's Kingdom? But Jesus' life was not all positive. He was hated by the Pharisees and Sadducees. They were continually trying to trap Him in doing or saying something that contradicted the Old Testament. Jesus was also threatened with stoning several times, but He managed to escape because it was not His time to die.

But alas, an even darker day was coming for Jesus, a day He had known would come since the foundation of the world. He would have to die for the sins of the world. But His death would not be quick and painless. It would be agonizingly painful. Jesus wrestled with the knowledge of what was coming. He had to prepare His disciples as well as Himself for the events that would shortly take place. Jesus had been giving them glimpses of what His last days would look like for nine months before He went to the cross.

But the idea of the Messiah dying was not what they had pictured in their minds. They had the vision of the conquering king who would come and make all nations bow before Him. Unfortunately, the disciples had mistakenly thought Jesus' first coming was what the Old Testament referred to as His second coming. At Jesus' second coming, He will come in the clouds, and He will set up His Kingdom as an actual government here on Earth. All of the kings of the Earth will bow before Him as the one who rules over all the nations of the Earth.

Instead, in obedience to the Father, Jesus gave the disciples a new model of understanding true leadership as He bowed down and washed the disciples' feet. He was modeling a kind of leadership that was completely counter-cultural. This new way to lead was to prepare them to go out and reap a great harvest, leading toward His second coming. After washing their feet, they sat and enjoyed their last meal together. Having taught them, performed miracles, lived with them, Jesus had only to break bread with them one last time. As He broke the bread and took the cup, He was showing them His final gift of obedience, the cross. Jesus came in obedience to live and to die in order that we would have an example of how to take up our own cross and follow Him.

Jesus' final act of obedience was the most difficult of all. Even though Jesus was fully God, He was also fully man. Being a man meant that He would experience the fullness of the pain; He would bear the fullness of the world's sin. Paul writes it so beautifully, *"He who knew no sin became sin for us that we might become the righteousness of God in Him"* (2 Corinthians 5:21). It was this goal of bringing us into His Father's Kingdom that gave Jesus the fortitude and strength to press on despite the scorn and the shame.

In the Garden of Gethsemane, Jesus wrestled with the task before Him. Though He knew this was the reason He had come to Earth, He still asked the Father if there would be another way to bring about the salvation of the world, pleading for Him to *"take this cup away from Me"* (Luke22:42). But He humbled Himself before the Father and said if there was no other way, then He would go to the cross (Luke 22:42). But Jesus was in agony as He wrestled with the challenges that were before him. Luke writes, *"And being in agony, He prayed more earnestly. Then His sweat became like great drops of blood falling down to the ground"* (Luke 22:44). His calling was to bear the stripes, the humiliation, the shame as He walked through the streets carrying His cross. He bore it all in order for us to be in relationship with the Father.

Jesus' obedience was complete. As He was taken from the garden, He did not utter a word in His defense. He did not try to get out of the chains that bound Him or choose with a word to take down those holding Him prisoner. As a sheep before the slaughter, He quietly suffered not only physically with the 40 lashes they gave Him with shards of bone or metal tied to the end of the whip, tearing His flesh, but He did not make a sound, not one complaint, fulfilling His obedience to the prophetic word (Isaiah 53:7). He also endured the humiliation of the soldiers spitting on Him, mocking Him with the crown of thorns (Isaiah 53:5) He was obedient to the very end. Completely broken for our sin.

A Constant Choice

Our obedience is not a onetime choice when we become saved. Rather, it is continually choosing the life Christ has chosen for us to walk. We have to continually see with eyes of faith. Even though there are many good options for us to choose, only one choice aligns with the heart of the Father. The choice of obedience does not always lead to success in ministry or more wealth or a promotion at work. But it does always lead us closer to Him, becoming more conformed to the image of Christ in our daily lives. Obedience does lead to the blessings of more of His presence, greater revelation of His word, a deeper intimacy as we move about our day, an unhindered ability to hear His voice speaking to us, and an increased fascination with His beauty and glory.

In Moses' last speech to the Israelites, he was firmly convinced of the importance of obedience in following the Lord. As he was about to go up to the top of Mount Nebo and die, he wanted to share with the Israelites one last time, leaving a lasting impression upon them of the absolute necessity of full and complete obedience. Maybe because he had experienced the overwhelming rebuke from the Lord regarding his own disobedience, he wanted them to understand that the only way to move forward in God is through obedience to Him. Near the end of his sermon, he says,

> "See, I have set before you today life and good [obedience], death and evil [disobedience], in that I command you today to love [to love is to obey] the Lord your God, to walk in His ways, and to keep [obey] His commandments, His statutes, and His judgments, that you may live and multiply; and the Lord your God will bless you in the land which you go to possess. But if your heart turns away so that you do not hear, and are drawn away, and worship other gods and serve them, I announce to you today that you shall surely perish"
> Deuteronomy 30:15-18

Contemplation:

As we reflect on how we are doing in the area of obedience, when we sense the Lord asking us to do something, we need to ask ourselves if we walk away and do not do it, or do it though begrudgingly, or struggle with whether to obey or not, or immediately say yes. We would all love to be in the category of immediately saying yes. However, if we are not honest with ourselves and our posture in this area, then we cannot grow.

1. Take some moments to listen to the Lord. Ask the Holy Spirit to show you some instances of disobedience. Confess those times of disobedience and ask the Lord to fill you with the spirit of instantaneous obedience that Jesus had. Ask the Lord to remove from your heart every hindrance to complete obedience, whether excuses, lies, distractions or anything else. Praise the Lord for His goodness and willingness to help us to choose obedience every time.

2. What is something concerning obedience that is new or something the Holy Spirit is highlighting? Take the insight the Lord is highlighting and share it with someone else. Challenge someone else in their walk with the importance of loving the Lord through our obedience to His voice and His ways.

Prayer:

Father, I know You give good gifts to Your children. I ask for the immediate "yes" to arise in my spirit when I sense You are asking me to do something. Come and fill me with the joy that comes from obediently following Your ways and Your calling. Make me a vessel whom You can trust to always obey Your voice and move confidently in following after You all my days. I want to be able to finish my journey well in full obedience to Your commandments. In Jesus' name I pray, AMEN.

PART II:
Habits of the Abandoned Devotion Lifestyle

The first part of this book looked at the inward movements of our heart in the *abandoned devotion lifestyle* as we move through our journey with the Lord. These movements of our inner life do not necessarily always progress neatly from one stage to the next, but these movements are each key to growing in abandoned devotion. As we practice the movements and choose to be intentional about our development in them, we will begin to see growth in our wholehearted love for the Lord.

Another key in our development is the understanding of a lifetime perspective of growing in God and choosing to be faithful in our walk with Him. We are not sprinting in a 100-meter dash, but the Lord is developing His image inside of us through the endurance and perseverance of a marathon race. He wants us to trust Him in ever-deepening ways that challenge our faith to go beyond what we have trusted Him for previously. His primary goal is for us to cultivate a rich understanding of His character and His ways that continually leads us to obediently follow Him wherever He calls us. The richness of this means we grasp His love a little bit now, but throughout the course of our lifetime He is continually deepening our understanding and revealing more of the width, length, height and depth of God's love.

While the most important part of the *abandoned devotion lifestyle* is listening to the Holy Spirit and being obedient in what He is asking of us—whether that is repentance, more faith, or helping us to have His character inside of us—we also must actively participate in the abandoned devotion lifestyle. This active participation includes habits that will stimulate our growth as well as keep us steadfast no matter what storm or desert we face. Although these habits are foundational, their simplicity speaks to the nature of our relationship with God. Some people try to make life with God complicated when in fact it is simply a relationship of listening and responding, sharing and enjoyment, comfort and love.

These habits need to be a consistent part of our daily life in order for us to experience the fullness of God's presence in our lives. If we stray from these for too long, we will experience a distance in our relationship with God. Any relationship must be nurtured and cultivated with communication and time spent in the presence of one another. Without these, every relationship will suffer, and our relationship with the Lord is no different. We cannot expect the intimacy of deep relationship with God without these habits being present on a daily basis.

We will look at four habits that will help us to communicate and spend time in His presence. These tools are essential for our lifelong development as true disciples. First, we will look at studying God's Word. While this seems basic, it is a key to going deeper than merely a devotional reading of God's Word. We want more understanding related to principles of God's Kingdom and to knowing how God operates in different situations. Second, we will look at prayer as the key means of communication in the life of a true disciple. We are not talking about reading a list to God, but rather cultivating an intimate and deep communication within a relationship. Third, we will look at the habit of fasting. Fasting is a key tool that Jesus tells us to use as an instrument of bringing forth His Kingdom here on Earth. Finally, the last habit involves our awareness of spiritual warfare. This habit is not one we enter into lightly, but a necessary part of advancing Christ's Kingdom here on Earth. The enemy does not want to see Christ's disciples sharing the good news and multiplying themselves around the world; so, as a result, he will stop at nothing to compel us to give up and go home.

6

Studying God's Word

This first habit of the *abandoned devotion lifestyle* may seem too basic at first glance, but the Lord does not want us to just glance over His Word in the morning or just read it to check it off the list of things to do. The Lord wants to speak to us through His Word. He wants us to experience the dynamic interaction with His Spirit as we read the Word and hear the Spirit speaking to us, highlighting words and phrases, unlocking truth in our hearts that will set us free. Some may come to this phrase "studying God's Word" and assume it is just for pastors or teachers, but it is not for them. However, Christ has made His Word available to every believer purposefully to release understanding and revelation to each heart that reads it.

Importance of Studying God's Word

In the first part of this book, we began by talking about wanting to know more of God and to understand His character and His ways. We cannot grow in our understanding of God and His ways apart from studying His Word. It takes more than simply reading a verse or even memorizing a verse. We need to read the Scripture and then ask ourselves, "What is this passage teaching me about God's character?" "What does this passage teach me about how God interacts with my sinful nature?" "What does this passage teach me about His ways of bringing healing and freedom to His people?"

1. Our study of God's Word increases our hunger to know Him more.

God desires for us to go deeper and search His Word. We cannot be casual about our relationship with God. We have to be intentional to carve out time to lay hold of the fullness God wants to give us of Himself. God promises when we search for Him with wholehearted devotion we will find Him. He will reveal more of Himself to us. The prophet Jeremiah writes, *"And you will seek Me and find Me, when you search for Me with all your heart"* (Jeremiah 29:13). The prize of truly knowing God does not go to those who are content with reading a Scripture here or there or even for those who read their Bibles faithfully every morning but never take time to reflect on what they are learning and how it should change the way they live.

Searching is deliberate. Searching comes out of desperation. When my kids come home from school, the first thing they do is go straight to the kitchen. Out of hunger and desperation, they begin searching the whole kitchen for some bit of food to fill their hungry bellies. If we are so satisfied with other things in our lives, we will not make the time to search out the Scriptures and listen to what the Spirit is saying. We are called to live hungry, and the more we study the Scriptures, the more hungry we become. We are called to live searching, seeking, knocking because those who seek Him will find Him.

2. Studying God's Word increases our hatred of sin.

Second, our study of God's Word enables us to grow in our hatred of sin. As we study God's Word, we develop our understanding of what is truly sin before God. Sin is not just the ugly, awful public crimes that are plastered all over the news—a man was murdered, a woman stole something, this man raped these women. Sin is everywhere, and it is easy to see the heinous sin nature at work around the world. But it is much harder to discern attitudes of the heart.

Studying God's Word reveals to us the secret sins of our hearts which either we like to cover up or which the world actually encourages. Reflecting back on the passage of Scripture we read earlier about Saul, he was overcome by the need to please people instead of God. This people-pleasing spirit is not always easily detectable when we first meet someone. Our inward motivations are hidden from the vast majority of people around us, but God wants the entirety of our hearts. He does not want us to live to please other people. He is jealous over our lives and our hearts and wants us fully devoted to Him.

Our study of Scripture brings to light these hidden motives and secret sins and allows the Holy Spirit to blow a spirit of conviction over that area in order to draw us to repentance. A.W. Pink highlights the need to understand the Spirit's conviction in our lives through the Word, not just to draw us toward conversion but as a daily experience of the mature believer. He writes, "Such conviction that brings home to the heart the awful ravages which sin has wrought in the human constitution is not to be restricted to the initial experience which immediately precedes conversion."[8] This awareness of our sin will grow as we remain faithful to study His word and rely on His Spirit to teach us and lead us into truth. God does not want us to remain in the dark, trapped in sin, on the outside of His presence looking in. He desires for us to see our sin, confess it to Him and enter the Holy Place of His Presence. Studying His Word enables us to do this and therefore experience a deeper measure of His Presence in our lives.

3. Our study of God's Word reveals how we should live.

Third, we gain greater insight into how He intends for us to live. Often, for those who are new to the faith, they do not always know how they should live. As those who are discipling them, it is essential we are leading them back to God's Word for them to be able to discern what living as Christ's disciple looks like. We do not necessarily need to tell them what to do but to encourage them to go and search the Scriptures or suggest a Scripture for them to read as they wrestle with their question about what to do.

There are many questions related to life in today's world that God's Word does not necessarily speak about directly. However, God's Word is living and active and sharper than any two-edged sword. His living Word is able to speak directly to our situation without speaking directly about the circumstances we are facing. I cannot begin to count the number of times the Lord has spoken to me through His Word about a situation I was facing through a verse that had nothing to do with my circumstances. Yet, God's application of that verse brought insight and guidance for how to move forward. We cannot limit the God of the universe. He is infinitely able to speak if we will go to His Word and listen for His voice speaking to us.

4. Studying God's Word intensifies our love and devotion for Him.

Fourth, we intensify our love and devotion to Him as we study the Word of God. Reading and studying God's Word brings the fire of God into our walk with Him. We study His Word and stand amazed at His providence, His kindness, His love, and our amazement leads to fascination with His character and His beauty. We are consumed with a desire to know more and go deeper. The more we understand of the great lengths to which He has gone to save us and deliver us from our oppression, the more our love for Him grows.

Reading and studying God's Word will also sustain our love and devotion through the dry periods in our life. We all go through seasons where it seems we cannot hear God as well as we could before or maybe we do not hear Him speaking at all. Because we do not hear Him speaking, we think His love for us has grown cold as well. We go to our prayer closets, and we pour out our hearts to God, but all we know is silence. It seems as if God has hidden Himself from us, and we cannot figure out how to get back to that place of hearing His voice and experiencing that deep intimacy we once had.

During these times, it is easy to stop reading God's Word because it is not as exciting as it was before when God was speaking to us. The habit we once found truly inspiring as we connected with the God of the universe now seems dull, a bit boring, and we sometimes wonder why we spend our time doing it when we do not get anything out of it. However, these are just lies the enemy wants us to believe. The truth is the Word of God is living and active even when it seems like the words are dead. As we read the Bible, we may not feel touched in our emotions, but our spirit is being fed living truth to keep us walking in the right direction. Without continually going back to the fountain to be renewed by God's words of truth, we can easily get off track and start believing things that are actually lies.

The Bible is more than just a book written by a bunch of people over the centuries. It is words, inspired by God, to bring healing and hope, life and love, faith and forgiveness to each person who reads it. God's Word is our lifeline to the Father. When you are desperate and do not know where else to turn, turn to God's Word. Ask Him to speak. Listen for His answer. He is really never far from us, but is always patiently waiting for us to run into His arms of love once again.

5. Those who are faithful disciples are called to teach others. Studying God's Word prepares us for this responsibility in Christ's Kingdom.

As disciples whom Jesus has called, we are now entrusted with the responsibility to teach others what we have learned. This is not just for pastors and ministry leaders. Jesus expects every believer to be studying His Word in order to be able to teach others what He is saying. Only as we are faithful to study God's Word will we be ready to fulfill Christ's command to teach others to do the same. Inherent in the nature of the good news is something to be shared. In the Sermon on the Mount, Jesus says to His disciples,

> "Whoever therefore breaks one of the least of these commandments,and teaches men so, shall be called least in the kingdom of heaven, but whoever does and teaches them, he shall be called great in the kingdom of heaven" (Matthew 5:19).

We are not meant to keep it all to ourselves, but we are called to take it and share it with our neighbors, our co-workers, and our community. This phrase "teaching others" does not mean everyone in the body of Christ is to become a teacher of God's Word in order to be faithful and fulfill God's calling. However, we are all expected to be sharing with someone what we are learning. Because God speaks to us in many ways, what you share could be something the Lord highlighted to you in a book you are reading or maybe a Scripture He used to ask you to do something. The key is to talk about it with someone else because this increases our accountability to what God is speaking, and it invites others into the process of maturing and listening for what God is speaking to them.

This fundamental principle of communicating the blessing of truth that God has entrusted to us has been a cornerstone of the faith since the time of Abraham. When we look back at the Abrahamic covenant, we see a foundation of the faith – Abraham was blessed to be a blessing. We are not to just take the truths of the faith or the wonderful things God is speaking to us and become our own little holy huddle. Rather, we are to take the blessing we have been given and share it with someone else. We can see this so evidently throughout the Bible. God has spoken words to the prophets that we can still apply to our circumstances today. The letters Paul wrote to the churches he visited are now a guide for us as we grow in the faith. When we share it, God can multiply the blessing exponentially. We should be sharing the blessing out of the overflow of what we are reaping in our times with the Lord, an ever-increasing depth of knowledge and understanding of God's Word that we have put into practice in our own lives.

Sometimes, it can be scary to share what we have heard from God because it requires us to be vulnerable. Some things God speaks to us are things that we are to hide in our hearts and ponder. Usually, these are things about the future as with Mary pondering Jesus' future as the shepherds came and told her of angels' proclamation (Luke 2:19). The Lord was giving Mary insight into the fullness of what God would do through Jesus, but Mary did not yet understand it all. When we receive these kinds of words, it is important to continue to pray through it until understanding finally comes.

How to Study God's Word

An important tool for every believer is to be rooted in how to study God's Word. Anyone can read a bit of Scripture for their devotions and listen to what God is saying through them. However, God really wants us to go deeper in knowing and understanding His Word by studying it in depth. We want to have a solid grasp of the reason why God has included each book of the Bible. We are not called to do this in a year, but over the course of a lifetime we are constantly choosing books to study that will help us to grow in our calling and increase our devotion to God.

1. Select a Passage of Scripture

In this section, we will begin by giving a basic outline of steps to take as we study the Bible, and then we will take an example for study from the Bible as a way to see the application of the method we are using.

First, consider where to begin. This method of studying Scripture can be applied to any study of the Bible. So, we must first decide what we are going to study. When approaching Scripture, we can study a book of the Bible, which is helpful to see an overview of the whole as well as studying each passage in-depth. Another way of studying is to look at a particular passage of Scripture, which could be as small as a few paragraphs or a few chapters of a particular book where a theme connects those parts together. Another approach is to study Scripture from the point of view of looking at the life of a person. For example, the life of David spans several books of the Bible, but it is all connected under one theme.

2. Background of the Passage of Scripture – Author, Date and Context

Second, after we have selected the passage to study, we begin by looking at the background of this passage. We ask questions such as who wrote this passage of Scripture, when was it written, where was it written, what were the circumstances the author faced while writing this passage. This information will give us new insight into the words the author wrote and why. In the book of Philippians, Paul writes, **"Rejoice in the Lord always. Again I will say, Rejoice!"** (Philippians 4:4). This testimony Paul gives to always rejoice may seem a challenge in our everyday lives with the many opportunities for complaint and problems all around us. But it is even more powerful because he wrote this from a prison cell in Rome. He was not sitting on a hill, watching the sunset after a glorious day of ministering to thousands of people. He was sitting in a cell, hungry because the prisons did not feed their prisoners as they do today and very dirty from the horrible conditions in which he found himself. Yet, he did not resort to complaining and grumbling but rather chose joy in the midst of his turmoil. Considering the background of the author and the date in history it was written shed new light on the words we read. In the book of Isaiah, we find multiple passages of Scripture referring to Jesus' coming. These prophetic words were written 700 years before Jesus was born. The greatness of God is revealed as we marvel at His ability to give us glimpses of the signs of the times if we will only pay attention to what the Spirit is saying. Not only this, but God's plan of redemption was not hatched overnight in a desperate attempt to save a lost people. God knew the day was coming when He would intervene in the fabric of history to make a way for His beloved Son to save His Bride. God is a planner. Every detail of our lives is not happenstance or coincidence. God has a destiny for us, but we must engage with Him to see it come to pass. Do we see God's plan and providence in our own lives? Are we looking for it? We will miss it without the eyes of faith to ask the questions and see the plan God is orchestrating in our midst. When we dig into God's Word, we see these truths touch our spirit and bring life into our circumstances.

3. Audience

Next, we look at the audience or to whom the book or passage was written. The audience is another crucial piece that shapes the way we read what has been written. The author has crafted the message of the book with the help and direction of the Holy Spirit to speak to a particular group of people. We want to ask ourselves questions such as how the listener would have heard this message and what cues in the text make it easier for the listener to have understood.

A great example of the importance of the audience lies in reading the four gospels at the beginning of the New Testament. Here, we see four accounts of the same story. Jesus' life, death and resurrection are all presented in these four accounts. While there are many similarities in these four accounts, we also see some rather vivid differences. We can understand these differences based primarily on two reasons.

First, the author's perspective of these events is shaped by their own background, upbringing, relationship to Jesus, and purpose in writing the book. Second, these accounts are shaped by the audience to whom the author is writing.

For example, the gospel of Matthew has some of the same content as the gospels of Mark and Luke. However, Matthew has rearranged some of the content to emphasize Jesus' teaching ministry, forming five sermons that make up the framework of Matthew's gospel. Another reason for Matthew's arrangement in this fashion is because he is writing to a primarily Jewish audience. At the beginning of the gospel, Matthew showed through Jesus' lineage His Jewish roots. Through the framework of the book, he portrays Jesus as the King who has come to set up His Kingdom, and His first sermon outlines the constitution of His Kingdom. Matthew continues to develop Jesus as the great Teacher until His final sermon, where Jesus explains this is both the Kingdom that is now and not yet. Although Jesus has taught this before in His sermons, He is trying to prepare His disciples and followers for His impending death and resurrection that will usher in a new age of the church and bring forth an anticipation of His second coming.

In addition to the framework that portrays Jesus as the fulfillment of the Jewish Messiah, Matthew uses language particular to the Jewish community. John Lightfoot writes, "This is seen in his use of Jewish symbols, terms and numbers without explanation" (Commentary on Matthew). Matthew uses many references that Jews would understand. For example, in reference to Jerusalem, he uses "City of the great King," while in referencing Christ he uses the terms "Son of David" and "Son of Abraham." Matthew also uses the phrase that the "Scripture might be fulfilled." This clear picture Matthew paints of Jesus as the Jewish Messiah is at every point undergirded to reach his Jewish audience.

4. Read the Whole Passage at One Time

Next, after we have selected a passage or book of the Bible, we begin by reading the whole of what we are studying in one sitting. For some studies, this may be difficult as the subject is quite long, such as the book of Isaiah or studying the life of David. Therefore, it is advisable to start with a smaller section of study and work into the larger passages. By reading the whole passage in one sitting, the reader is able to firmly grasp the overarching themes that hold the passage together. Each person has a method of learning that is best for them. Some people are more auditory, while others are visual. Because of the various learning styles, greater understanding might be gleaned from listening to the whole passage of Scripture read aloud. Others might find it beneficial to listen while they write notes or circle words as they read it. Interaction with the Scripture in multiple ways is helpful for giving us a better picture of what we are studying.

5. Select a Theme

Once we feel we have a solid grasp of the entirety of the book or passage, it is time to select a broad theme that encompasses the whole of the study. This does not limit us to talking about this theme only, but it gives us clarity and focus as we begin studying. It helps us to see the broad picture and how all of the pieces fit into that larger theme, bringing cohesion and continuity to our study. This theme also guides us in our interpretation of the pieces to make sure we are being faithful to the Scripture and not making the Scripture say something it does not. Many preachers easily take one verse and make a sermon out of it. However, taking one verse allows us to put our own interpretation and meaning upon that verse, which was never intended by the Holy Spirit. Reading the context and delving into the background of the text guards us from making the Scripture say something which it does not.

6. Research Other Texts with Similar Phrases

In order to study the Bible well, we need to compare and contrast what we see in the Scripture we are studying in light of other Scriptures with similarities. Within the Bible, we rarely see something said only once. Through the inspiration of the Holy Spirit, we see themes continually recurring throughout the Old and New Testaments. The way these themes are displayed in the lives of the people of God is unique, but the subject often remains the same. Whether we were to read a text about God's mercy or a theme like the "Day of the Lord," these important messages are continually highlighted throughout the Word of God.

God is in the business of giving us multiple opportunities to learn from things in the past to better understand God's dealings with us now and His coming Kingdom that He will establish. We see this with the 10 plagues in Egypt. These plagues were a type or shadow that gives us a depth of understanding as we look to the end of the age in Revelation and see the seven trumpets and seven bowls of judgment. In the Old Testament prophets, many of them refer to this "Day of the Lord," and each of them give perspectives revealed by the Holy Spirit which when put together give us greater understanding. In the gospels, we often have at least two retellings of events that happened during the ministry of Jesus by comparing the accounts in each of the gospels. When we put these different accounts together, we come to a more complete understanding of what Jesus really intends for us as His disciples.

In the Sermon on the Mount, Jesus very explicitly tells His disciples He had a deeper level of meaning He intended for them in the Ten Commandments, but they were hard of heart and did not understand. Jesus says, *"You have heard it said of old…, but I say to you."* Jesus is not giving new commandments. Rather He is explaining that the Ten Commandments were not a list of rules to follow, but they were intended to be a roadmap for where to guard our hearts. When we compare the Ten Commandments, such as do not murder, with Jesus' admonition to not be angry, we see a greater revelation of what He originally intended in the Ten Commandments. Jesus highlights first the similarity of the importance of not murdering. The same commandment given to Moses is the same commandment today. However, Jesus wants His disciples to understand the root of murder.

The Father knew our hearts would be tempted by anger. Therefore, He commanded us not to murder, but the root of murder is our temptation to easily get angry. These comparisons with other Scriptures give us a greater understanding of what Jesus is saying. As we see these side by side, we also see the contrasts of what makes each writer's perspective unique. This is also helpful as these contrasts bring depth to our reading of God's Word. God has made each of us unique, and He incorporates these perspectives to give a greater revelation of Himself. God cannot be limited to one person's opinion. It is only as we, as the body of Christ collectively come together to study and share with one another that we can see multiple perspectives and grasp a greater understanding of God's Word.

7. Break the Passage into Sections

Within a given passage of Scripture, it is best to begin by breaking the whole into smaller sections. After we have read the whole passage several times, we will begin to see where the natural breaks are in the passage. It is sometimes not where we see a chapter number or even where we see a break or section in our Bible. These chapter numbers and breaks were not in the original text. Therefore, we must read it altogether to see where it naturally divides. If we are studying a larger book of the Bible like the book of Acts, then we would begin by dividing it into larger sections encompassing several chapters each. Then, each of these sections could be further broken down to smaller sections for easier study. The key for dividing the passage into sections is to find what connects the different parts. In the book of Acts, Luke follows two main people, though others are mentioned: Peter and Paul. Therefore, we could divide the book at Acts 12:24 being the end of Peter and the other disciples' ministry after Pentecost and Acts 12:25 until the end as Paul's journeys spreading the good news. Other commentators have divided it into three sections. These different perspectives should not cause us to be perplexed by needing to find the right answer. As long as we are listening to the Holy Spirit, we will be guided in our interpretation. It is helpful to read many commentaries that can be easily found online for free. It is essential we do not become isolated in our interpretation but to find as many resources as we can to understand God's Word and His meaning. We gain more clarity as we read more perspectives.

Another example of dividing the Scripture we are reading into sections is to look at the Sermon on the Mount in Matthew 5-7. This particular passage of Scripture is frequently broken into several smaller narratives and often preached in isolation from one another. However, the importance of sub-dividing this sermon becomes critical to the implications of the passage. As we read through the first part of chapter 5, we see the commonly referred to Beatitudes. These Beatitudes are often preached on their own. But alas, the reader misses the reference to the Beatitudes found in the following verses. Jesus says, *"You are the salt of the earth, but if the salt loses its flavor, how then shall it be seasoned?"* (Matthew 5:13). This salt and flavor Jesus refers to is what is produced through the cultivation of the Beatitudes. We cannot be salt in the Earth apart from these core realities.

These implications become even greater as we see the implication of this for the Great Commission. How can we then be light in the world? Only as we are cultivating these Beatitudes can we truly be effective in ministry. Effective ministry flows out of a fervent cultivation of Christ's image in us. Too easily in the Christian life, we become caught up with doing more and serving more. However, Christ cautions us to be aware of the tendency to lose our flavor if we do not continue to grow and develop these core realities in our lives. We are never going to be completely poor in spirit or meek, but we are committed in our lives to continually going deeper and growing more in this lifestyle. The moment we stop growing, we do not just plateau, but we actually begin to backslide and open ourselves to easily slip into sin.

8. Begin with the First Section and Go Verse by Verse

After having done the hard work of seeing the big picture, now we can go in-depth in our study of the Scripture line by line. As we do this in-depth approach, it is important to read many commentaries on what we are studying and gain various perspectives. We can use other helpful Bible tools such as dictionaries and concordances to do word studies, and these studies will bring greater understanding to the section we are studying. Though this requires work, the reward is well worth it. The Holy Spirit is faithful to highlight new things to us and give greater insight.

In the Sermon on the Mount, we can examine the rich meaning of the word "blessed," which Jesus uses repeatedly. Each of the Beatitudes has a rich meaning like being "poor in spirit," "meek," and "hungering and thirsting for righteousness." These rich word studies combined with the analysis of each verse through reading several different commentaries from various perspectives brings depth and understanding to our reading of God's Word.

9. Finally, Find the Application of the Scripture

Scripture is only as useful to us as how we are applying it to our lives and allowing the Word of God to shape us into the image of His Son. If we go into deep reading and studying God's Word but we fail to practice it, then we have not really gained anything. James writes, *"But be doers of the word, and not hearers only, deceiving yourselves"* (James 1:22). It is easy for us to deceive ourselves into thinking we are spiritual because we go to church and hear the Word preached. We think ourselves even more devoted when we sit at home and read our Bibles. Alas, without allowing the Word of God to transform us, we are no better than an unbeliever who hears the Word. We must be rooted in seeing how the Scripture connects to our everyday lives. The Holy Spirit is always available to help us and eager to tell us if we would ask and then listen, but it is often our busy schedules that keep us from spending the necessary time to reflect and apply what we are learning in the Scriptures.

Application:

If you have never done an in-depth study of God's Word, today is your day to begin. Start by choosing a small book of the Bible that you know you can finish. The hardest part of being a faithful student of God's Word is to make it a part of your day. It requires dedicated time set aside in your daily schedule. Otherwise, it will be easily overlooked or even forgotten. The first few times you may want to set an alarm in order to be reminded, but eventually you will look forward to your time in the Word.

Contemplation:

It is time to evaluate how you are doing in your study of God's Word. What is God speaking to you? What are the new things you are learning from God's Word? What are you studying right now in Scripture?

Now is the time to make a change. Now is the time to set your heart to go deeper in Scripture.

1. What is one book of the Bible you have always wanted to know more about? Maybe you want to start smaller and study one of the parables Jesus uses in the gospels. No matter what the Spirit is highlighting to you, the key is to start now. Do not put it off! Find the time to start today.

2. Find a friend who wants to read and study the passage of Scripture together and compare what you are finding as you read and study separately. This will keep you accountable as well as challenge someone else to deepen their faith through studying the Word in a deeper fashion.

Prayer:

Lord Jesus, I desire to go deeper in your Word. Holy Spirit, show me what you would have me study. Open my eyes to greater understanding and enliven my spirit to desire more of Your Word. Make Your Word a light to bring guidance and direction to my life and use it to reveal the wisdom of Your ways in my life. May my delight be in Your Word. In Jesus' name, Amen.

7

Prayer

Prayer is an essential habit for a believer to become a true disciple. Our communion with God is centered around this key discipline. In order for us to grow in our relationship with God, we must grow in prayer. Normally, our first experience in prayer is our prayer of repentance when we come to faith in Christ. Early in our walk with God, our prayers are often focused on ourselves and our need. This cry for God's help to overcome our sin nature and walk in victory is not only common but necessary. We challenge ourselves to resist the flesh and walk according to the Spirit as we depend upon God's enabling grace through prayer.

However, we are not called to be satisfied with simply focusing on ourselves or on our needs. It is easy for a believer to become stuck praying only for their needs, and can find themselves in a one-dimensional relationship with God. This one-way communication with God is all too common in the body of Christ. The Father is seen merely as One who gives us what we need when we ask. We see a need, so we pray and ask God to meet that need, but it is all about us and what we are going to get from it. There is a lack of true relationship in which we pray conversationally to receive understanding and insight into situations, asking the Lord what He is trying to teach us, hearing what is on the heart of the Father, and much more.

Prayer is the avenue for going deep with God. Looking back at the stages of progression in the first part of the book, we begin with brokenness as the entry point into deeper relationship with God. From there, we move into intimacy. Here, in the movement from brokenness to intimacy, we experience a shift in our prayer lives. The hungering and thirsting after God awaken in us a yearning to know God's Word and to hear His voice speaking to us. We are longing for more of God and to experience this reality in our everyday lives. Prayer is the way of unlocking this floodgate of deepening our experience with God.

As we move further in intimacy with God, we begin to rest in the place of beholding God, admiring Him for who He is, and enjoying His presence. We move from the place of always needing something to simply enjoying God for who He is. This movement is similar to what is experienced in the covenant of marriage. In the beginning of the marriage relationship, the couple is insecure about their relationship and therefore the needs have to be stated and repeated. But as the years go by, it becomes a safe place where one is known by the other. One spouse does not have to continually reiterate their needs because they have walked together for so long. The times together do not always have to be filled with words, but rather there is a deep enjoyment from being in the presence of the other.

This is the invitation to us as believers who are walking in covenant relationship with God. We are invited to behold and enjoy just being in His presence, standing in awe of His beauty and the goodness and faithfulness of His ways. In Psalm 27:4, we read David's words about his deep love for God and his enjoyment of beholding Him in His beauty. The one who is consistently beholding the Lord is being transformed as Paul writes, *"from glory to glory"* (2 Corinthians 3:18). Our perspective, reactions, responses and understanding are all changed as we set our eyes upon Him. As we behold God we become more like Him, transformed into His image and conformed into His likeness, where He increases and we decrease.

This meditative style of prayer – where we chew on God's Word and sit in the quietness of His presence – has in large part been lost in our world of instant gratification. If we do not experience some great revelation or vision in prayer, then we quickly write prayer off as not worth our time. But those who are only in prayer for the quick testimony and easy answers will never experience the deep rewards of waiting in God's presence, meditating deeply upon His word, and beholding Him in His beauty. We will also miss out on the answers to prayer we could have received had we laid hold of God's promises and continued in prevailing prayer until we saw God's work come to pass.

Not only does prayer take us deeper in our relationship with God, but it reveals another dimension of the Father's heart where He invites us to partner with Him through prayer. This dimension of wholehearted mutual partnership is the core reality of how the Lord intends for us to live our lives. The Lord desires for us to enter into partnership with Him with our whole heart, holding nothing back. He wants our partnership with Him to be mutual. "Prayer is essentially a partnership of the redeemed child of God working hand in hand with God toward the realization of His redemptive purposes on earth." [9] He reveals to us His plans, and we partner with Him by praying those plans into being. We cooperate through obeying what He wants us to do and praying exactly what we are supposed to pray. Our partnership with the Lord is matched by God's partnership with us. His faithfulness to bring forth His promises never fails.

Although the Lord is sovereign, He deliberately chooses to limit Himself by waiting for us to participate in His plan through partnership. John Wesley aptly writes, "God does nothing but in answer to prayer." [10] Wesley is not the only one to write this sentiment over the ages. E.M. Bounds, renowned theologian on prayer, writes, "The prayers of God's saints are the capital stock of heaven by which Christ carries on His great work upon the earth."[11] These great men of faith are ones who have seen the great mystery of God's Kingdom unfolding through the power of prayer on the Earth.

Similarly, we see the importance of prayer in the lives of countless message bearers throughout the centuries of mission history. Examples of faithful intercessors as message bearers abound, such as the hundred-year prayer meeting of the Moravians that catapulted a huge mission force into the unreached people groups around the world. We also see faithful message bearers like John Hyde, commonly referred to as "Praying Hyde" because of his commitment to pray and asked the Lord for souls each day before he would even go out and talk to one person; and David Brainerd, whose commitment to prayer brought forth a mighty revival among Native Americans. These stories of old are repeated in corners of the world today. Friends of ours in Djibouti serving as message bearers had preached the gospel for years with very little fruit, but now, through faithful teammates engaged in prayer, breakthrough has come and many have come to faith. Similarly, in the Middle East, friends have seen places that have been resistant to the gospel message now experiencing a hungering and thirsting for living water like never before.

Throughout the course of church history, we see this pattern of people praying before revival breaks forth. In the Welsh revival, stories of small groups of men and women committing themselves to prayer preceded the outpouring of these major moves of God. Hungering for more of God, John and Charles Wesley and George Whitfield along with about 60 others celebrated New Year's by having a feast and prayer in 1739. As they continued in prayer, they were overcome with God's presence, crying out in joy; the power of God caused many to fall to the ground and finally all of them broke into song in one accord. [12] This event of waiting in prayer and the subsequent outpouring of the Spirit had such a profound impact upon Wesley and Whitfield that they were filled with the Holy Spirit and power. Not only had they experienced this power, but they hungered for God to pour out this same power and manifestation of the Spirit around the world. During the Finney revivals, Wesley Duewel recounts one experience Finney had in Utica, N.Y.

"After some twenty days, Finney went to Utica to attend a funeral. He found a godly lady who had been prevailing in prayer almost incessantly for two days and nights. One of the Presbyterian pastors asked him to come back to Utica to speak. He returned almost at once. 'The Word took immediate effect, and the place became filled with the manifest influence of the Holy Spirit.'" [13]

Having tasted of God's Spirit being poured out, Finney longed for God to do it again. We cannot hunger and long for something we have never tasted. We have to earnestly seek God for this outpouring. It will not come to the casual passersby. It will not happen to those who are too busy to pray. God's Spirit is poured out on those who are giving of their time and attention to seek God in their context. God always desires to pour out more of Himself, but He is waiting to find those who are prepared to receive His coming and who are actively engaging with Him. Our partnership with Him is what brings what is possible into reality.

In John 2, Mary, the mother of Jesus, went to a wedding in Cana, and Jesus and the disciples were also invited to attend. During the festivities, they ran out of wine. Mary said to Jesus, "They have no wine," (verse 3) clearly expecting Jesus to do something to remedy the situation. Obviously, Mary would not have expected such a thing if she had not already seen Jesus do these things in her own home. Mary's confident expectation that Jesus was able to make something happen is contradictory to Jesus' statement that His time had not yet come. Is Mary wrong to expect Jesus to do something? Is Jesus wrong that this was not His time? No! But it is Mary's faith and confident assurance in Jesus that brought forth the miraculous into this situation. Mary partnered with Jesus. She called the stewards to do exactly as Jesus said, no matter how crazy it sounded. Her faith in Jesus brought what was impossible in the natural into reality through her dependence upon Jesus. Mary pulled forth what was not supposed to happen yet because she believed and persevered. Even though it was not yet the time, Jesus answered because of Mary's faith and confident assurance of Jesus' power to breakthrough natural circumstances to bring about extraordinary results. This gives us a picture of what God is asking of us related to prayer. He wants us to partner with Him in prayer to see what is naturally impossible come into reality through our confident expectation with the prayer of faith.

This small sampling of events throughout history barely begins to recount the extraordinary ways God has partnered with His people through prayer to pour out His presence, power and salvation for many. While these are events where we can tangibly see the connection between prayer and events in our midst, there are many saints throughout the centuries who have been instrumental prayer warriors who have faithfully obeyed the call to prayer and have labored not seeing the results of their prayers. Our responsibility to be faithful is not hinged upon seeing God move. We must be prepared to continue to cry out to God for those things that He is showing us, even when we are not seeing them come to pass.

Called to Partner in Prayer

Some people think partnering with God in prayer is only for those who are prayer warriors. They do not understand this call to partnership is for every believer. The Lord desires to release His plans and purposes into the body of Christ. God has designed prayer as the avenue through which these plans and purposes are released.[14] God is not looking only to those who are prayer warriors, but He is looking for those who are serious about prayer. Five minutes in prayer will not position us to receive insight and revelation from the Lord. Rather, we are called to a lifestyle of continuing in His presence through prayer.

From the moment we awake in the morning until we go to sleep at night, we are invited into a continual fellowship with the Holy Spirit. Making the choice to say "yes" to the invitation is the most difficult part. When we awake in the morning, we can say, "Good morning, Holy Spirit! I invite you to speak to me throughout the day and interrupt me at any time." Then, throughout our day, we seize the moments to go deeper in prayer. Maybe it is our practice to have time in the early morning for extended prayer. This is a great way to begin our day, but the conversation does not have to end there. We can talk to the Lord as we go about our day, whether in the menial tasks of life like washing dishes or ironing clothes, or in the time spent driving from one place to another. Every moment is an opportunity to engage with God in prayer. All of our days are structured differently, but no matter what your schedule is we must purposefully engage with God to hear His heart.

God has an abundance of things He wants to talk with us about, but it is often our limited schedule of time with Him which confines or restricts His ability to speak to us. Instead, we need to open up our whole day as a day spent with God, just as if we spent the day with our best friend doing the normal schedule of going to work together, having lunch together, and eating dinner together. Wouldn't our day seem much more exciting even if it was just the same schedule – but we were able to do it together? God wants to do everything with us rather than be pushed into a corner of our schedule and then be forgotten.

Beginning in Silence

To receive from the Lord, we have to be ready and listening. Sometimes, getting quiet to listen is the hardest part of prayer. We sit down for our quiet time, and the moment we close our eyes a thousand details about our day rush into our mind clamoring for our attention and work. We are desperately aware of our need to attend to the mountain of things on our to-do list, but we have to push through the voices, laying down the cry of the urgent, so we can hear the still small voice of the Lord speaking to us.

Some helpful strategies for finding that quiet space include speaking to the other voices in our minds and silencing them in the name of Jesus. The voices of our flesh are often those feelings of doubt, insecurity, guilt and fear. If we allow these voices to arise in our hearts unchecked and unchallenged by the Word of God, then we start to believe the doubts and insecurities and accept them as truth. These voices of self-talk lead to paralyzing behavior for some believers who have not taken the word of God and applied it to these situations and thoughts.

Another voice we often hear speaking to us is Satan's. We can identify Satan's voice because he is a liar and twists the truth. When we hear someone say something that has a hint of truth in it, but we sense there is also something not quite right about it, that is the enemy. Satan is also called the accuser of the brethren. When we want to lay the blame on someone else, we need to identify this as the enemy trying to destroy our relationships with others. This does not mean that we cannot or should not confront another brother or sister in the body of Christ when they have done something wrong. However, the spirit with which we confront someone is what is important. We should not come with the spirit of accusation, but rather a spirit of reconciliation that brings unity to the body of Christ. If our hearts are filled with offense, then our conversation will only create more problems. Instead, when we come earnestly trying to repair the breach, then we will find peace. Even if the other person does not respond in a way that restores relationship, we will find peace knowing we have done what the Lord asked of us.

The path of freedom begins with recognizing what is our flesh speaking and what is God's voice. Just as well as one knows the voice of their parents or spouse, so, too, we should know the voice of the Father speaking to us. It is very easy for us to accept our feelings as facts. We feel a certain way, and therefore we act. Rather, we must begin by examining our feelings and asking why we feel like that and what does the Bible say about those feelings. Once we have determined what lies beneath our feelings, only then can we rightly respond. We can also lay hold of the distractions like our "to-do" list by writing it down and laying it aside. God's voice always aligns with His Word. God's voice always brings peace. God's voice always exalts Jesus and not ourselves.

Sometimes, the problem is not the distractions but the emptiness of sitting in the quiet before the Lord. In our world of constant noise and social media, quiet can seem uncomfortable. Silence can almost be abrasive to our senses. In the silence, it can be helpful to meditate on a single verse and just read it over and over, asking the Lord to bring deeper revelation and understanding from His word. This process will bring focus to our silence and meditation that will help our minds avoid wandering from thought to thought.

As we quiet the thoughts and words of our mouth filled with our own needs and wants, the Lord fills the silence with His own plans, purposes and desires. These thoughts and desires surround not only our own circumstances, but the Lord also enlarges our heart in concern for those whom we have never met and maybe never will. The thrust of the gospel is consistently looking outward to how we can help and serve others. As Jesus was ministering to the multitudes, His heart was continually moved with compassion. In response to their need, Jesus multiplied the loaves and fishes, taught them God's truth, healed their diseases.

As we consider prayer as partnership with God, we need to first look at the requirements to enter into that partnership. Does God allow anyone to partner with Him? Yes! Any believer who is willing to meet His requirements can partner with Him to see His Kingdom come and His will be done here on Earth as it is in heaven. Often, our availability is what qualifies us in God's eyes. Being available is to set aside time to wait upon God and listen to Him. Beyond just a willingness, let's look at the requirements for those seeking to partner with God.

Necessary Keys for Effective Prayer

1. Humility

First, God is looking for those who know they need God to accomplish His plans and purposes in the Earth. Andrew Murray writes, "Humility is not so much a grace or virtue along with others; it is the root of all, because it alone takes the right attitude before God, and allows Him as God to do all."[15] Our prayer becomes not about us but seeing the greatness of God alone. E.M. Bounds writes, "Humility is an indispensable requisite of true prayer. ... That which brings the praying soul near to God is humility of heart. That which gives wings to prayer is lowliness of mind. That which gives ready access to the throne of grace is self-depreciation. Pride, self-esteem, and self-praise effectually shut the door of prayer."[16] We have to be careful of pride creeping into our lives. We can easily begin to depend upon our own effort and work to accomplish the task rather than the blessing of God. If we are so busy doing what God has asked us to do that we do not have time to pray, then we have not embraced humility.

Humility is key to rightly relating with God in prayer. We read in James, *"God resists the proud, but gives grace to the humble"* (James 4:6). God cannot answer the prayers of those who pray from a prideful heart. If we are not experiencing answered prayer, then we should begin by checking our hearts for pride. We must understand our desperate need for God and His unique ability to move in our situation. Convinced of our inability to produce lasting fruit without God, we cry out in humility and expectation for God to move.

2. Holiness

Partnership with God in prayer requires us to walk in holiness before Him in order to enter that secret place. Anyone can pray and ask God to move in their life. But true partnership with God in prayer where God reveals His plans and purposes and gives us wisdom and insight into how to accomplish these things only comes as we walk according to His ways. This is why the *abandoned devotion lifestyle* couples walking rightly before God in brokenness as a key movement to connect to our prayer lives. E.M. Bounds writes on prayer, "It is intense and profound business that deals with God and His plans and purposes, and it takes wholehearted men to do it. No half-hearted, half-brained, half-spirited effort will do for this serious, all-important, heavenly business."[17] We cannot live however we want and then expect for God to meet with us in prayer. Cheap grace is tempting, but it is incompatible with the lifestyle of partnering with God in prayer.

In Genesis 18, we read in the story of Sodom and Gomorrah how the Lord chooses to share with Abraham what He is going to do. This fascinating story is especially insightful because in it we see God sharing with us His prerequisites for sharing His plans with someone. These verses tell us how God thinks! The Lord said, *"Shall I hide from Abraham what I am doing?"* (v. 17). The Lord is looking for the right people with whom He can share His plans and purposes. He is looking for those who would be faithful with His desires and fulfill His plans and not their own. This intimate wording reminds us of how one would talk to their spouse. Should I hide this thing from my best friend? The intimacy we discussed earlier in this book is the same expectation God has for those who would enter into the place of partnering with Him in prayer.

Then, God says, *"For I have known him, in order that he may command his children and his household after him, that they keep the way of the Lord, to do righteousness and justice, that the Lord may bring to Abraham what He has spoken to him"* (Genesis 18:19). Here we see two things. First, Abraham was committed to keeping the way of the Lord. His heart was set upon obeying God and his commandments, living a holy life before God. Yet, the Lord did not stop here. The Lord highlighted Abraham as faithful to teach those around him to obey God as well. Those who are faithfully following God will naturally be teaching those around them to obey God.

We see this same expectation communicated by Jesus in the Sermon on the Mount. Jesus said, *"Whoever therefore breaks one of the least of these commandments and teaches men so, shall be called least in the kingdom of heaven, but whoever does and teaches them, he shall be called great in the kingdom of heaven"* (Matthew 5:19). This is the nature of the gospel in true believers. We live in such a way as to outwardly draw others into the Kingdom. Our holiness should be contagious! We should be able to say to others as Paul did, *"Imitate me, just as I also imitate Christ"* (1 Corinthians 11:1). Our lives should be such a testimony to others that we are challenging others to live like Christ.

3. Partnering with God to See His Promises Fulfilled

God has called us into His heavenly Kingdom to be co-heirs with Christ. This position empowers us to partner with God. Jesus said to His disciples, *"No longer do I call you servants, for a servant does not know what his master is doing; but I have called you friends, for all things that I have heard from My Father I have made known to you"* (John 15:15). This awesome promise of deeper relationship is repeated throughout the New Testament in varying ways. We are no longer expected to stand on the sidelines of history, but we are called to enter into God's story and partner with Him to write the ending. He has plans and purposes for each one of us as part of our destiny in God. Through prayer, we are able to partner with Him to see these plans come to pass.

We read this same principle as a prerequisite in Abraham's life as well. God had initiated a covenant with Abraham, and this was the first occurrence of God marking His family on the Earth. Those in God's family are given these privileges of awesome responsibility. The Lord said of Abraham, *"Since Abraham shall surely become a great and mighty nation, and all the nations of the earth shall be blessed in him?"* (Genesis 18:18). God is stating the impracticality of not sharing with Abraham since God had given these promises to him – and when God promises something, it will definitely happen.

In Exodus 32, these same promises of God were a key to fighting for the destiny of Israel. The promises were both a prerequisite for coming into the secret place with God as well as the key to what Moses said before the Lord to turn back His wrath against the children. Because of the promises of God, the Lord had raised up a deliverer to bring the people out of Egypt. The Lord chose Moses to lead the people out of Egypt. In the wilderness, God continued to speak through Moses to shape the Israelites into His own people. The Lord led Moses up on the mountain and met with him face to face all because God was looking for someone to shepherd His people. In Exodus 32, after the people had been worshipping the golden calf, God was ready to still fulfill the promise but do it through Moses' lineage alone. But Moses reminded God of His promises to Abraham, Isaac and Jacob to multiply their descendants and give them the land as their inheritance. These precious promises to God's faithful servants reminded God to choose mercy and not utterly destroy all of the Israelites. They still received judgment for their sin (Exodus 32:35). Promises do not negate the consequences of our actions, but they do ensure a remnant will arise to fulfill the promise.

4. Boldness

Another key to entering into the place of partnership is boldness. We will not come into our destiny of crying out for nations by sitting on the sidelines, content to watch others prevail in prayer. Each one of us is given the opportunity to lay hold of the plans and purposes God is desiring to unfold in our lives. Each of us has equal access to God. But those who boldly enter the throne room of grace, who pursue God and don't let go until He answers, they will see answers to prayer that others forfeit because of their lack of boldness.

Going back to the story of Abraham, we see an opportunity set before him to intercede for the people of Sodom and Gomorrah. Abraham chose to draw near to the Lord and enter into the place of intercession. We can easily be distracted in our busy world today and miss the opportunity to draw near. God had a plan to destroy Sodom and Gomorrah, but He was looking for someone who would boldly enter into the throne room of grace and stand in the gap for those who had not known Him. In Isaiah 59, the Lord echoes this same idea. *"Then the Lord saw it, and it displeased Him that there was no justice. He saw that there was no man and wondered that there was no intercessor"* (Isaiah 59:15-16). God is looking for intercessors who would stand in the gap for those who are experiencing injustice, without a witness of the gospel, trapped in sin and bondage. Like the Israelites who were worshipping the golden calf, they needed an intercessor because God was ready to move on and make a new people for His own.

Dynamics of Partnering With God in Prayer

The following dynamics help us to see how prayer works and what are the keys to unlocking fruitfulness in our prayer lives. Oftentimes, people will begin in prayer, but the moment it becomes difficult, they quit. Understanding the dynamics of prayer will give us tools to go back to when our prayer did not get an easy answer. Seasons will come in life where we are called to wrestle with God and continue in the attitude of prayer until we see the heavens opened and the answer released.

1. Perseverance

The first and most important key to seeing God's purposes and plans released is to persevere in prayer. After we have entered into the place of partnering with God to see His plans and purposes come forth, we must choose to press the Lord for the fullness of what He intends to release. In the world today, many things come easily, almost instantaneously. We do not even have to go to the store to shop for what we need or want but just open up our computer and order it online. At the click of a button, we can have what we want delivered to our door. But the things of God do not happen quite so easily, and therefore many do not experience the fullness of what God has for them. We must prevail in prayer to see the fullness of God's plans and purposes released.

Prevailing prayer is prayer that refuses to let go of God until we see the answer to our prayers. Prevailing prayer is not casual in its outworking. Rather, it is purposeful, intentional and passionate. In George Muller's autobiography, he shared his reflection on the need for perseverance, "It is not enough to begin to pray, nor to pray aright; nor is it enough to continue for a time to pray; but we must patiently, believing, continue in prayer until we obtain an answer."[18] Prayer cannot be casual. Prayer must purposefully seek God for the answer with which He has burdened our hearts.

We see this type of prayer first with Abraham in his asking of the Lord again and again. Abraham did not let the Lord leave until he was sure God would answer. God would not have destroyed Sodom and Gomorrah if He had found only 10 righteous people. Abraham thought that just as he had taught his household to follow the ways of God and to walk in righteousness and justice, so, too, would Lot have taught his household. Alas, that was not the case. But still, in the midst of Abraham's cries for help and deliverance, the Lord saw Abraham's heart and his desire that Lot and his family would be saved. So, the Lord sent angels to rescue Lot and his family. Abraham prevailed in prayer, and the Lord answered and saved Lot and his family. God is desiring to pour out His grace and mercy if we will fervently seek His face.

Other examples of the need for persistence in prayer abound throughout Scripture. Jacob wrestled with the Angel until the blessing poured forth. Moses went back up on the mountain to intercede for the Israelites after their disobedience with the golden calf. Elijah had to pray seven times before he saw a cloud only as big as his fist appear on the horizon. These giants of the faith refused to be satisfied with praying once and not seeing the blessing of God revealed. They all chose to continue in prayer, wrestling and prevailing until the answer to their prayers came forth. Jesus even teaches the disciples in the

Sermon on the Mount to insistently ask in prayer. Jesus not only uses the present continuous tense in the Greek, *"ask and keep on asking,"* but He also emphasizes His point by saying, *"seek and keep on seeking,"* and *"knock and keep on knocking,"* using three different ways to repeat the same thing (Matt. 7:7). Jesus did not want us to miss His point.

Jesus also connected prayer to reaping the harvest. We are called to pray for God to send out laborers into the harvest fields. Andrew Murray writes, "The power which the Lord gives His people to exercise in heaven and earth is real; the number of laborers and the measure of the harvest does actually depend on their prayer."[19] Our co-labor with Christ through prayer is absolutely essential to seeing the Great Commission fulfilled. This could be the generation of the Lord's return if we will embrace this call to prevailing prayer to see all the nations worshipping before the Lord.

Another example of the perseverance necessary in intercession and partnership with God is found in Luke 18. As Jesus was teaching, He spoke this parable of the persistent widow to teach us to pray and not give up. She went to the unrighteous judge crying out for justice, and he gave it to her because she cried out night and day. Will we take our requests before the Righteous Judge and plead for His intervention? Will we intercede for those who do not know the way to Christ? Will we stand in the gap for those imprisoned in the chains of their bondage and confused by the religious ideologies that surround them? Will we cry out night and day? Will we give up our sleep? Will we devote our precious time during the day? Will we prevail in prayer?

2. Motivated by Our Understanding of God

Our intercession and partnership with God must be consistently motivated by our understanding of who God is. God is not Santa Claus, who gives out gifts to good girls and boys. God described His own nature as gracious and compassionate, slow to anger and rich in love (Exodus 34:6). It is this nature of God that motivates us to cry out to

God in intercession. He is longing to pour out His mercy. But without repentance, our sin requires judgment. Through intercession, we plead with God to draw people to repentance so the Lord can be gracious to them. We are overcome with God's compassion in intercession as we pray for those who are lost and scattered like sheep without a shepherd. As we not only understand God's nature, but also cultivate that same nature in ourselves, we then begin to cry out in intercession according to the Spirit working in our hearts.

We see this same motivation in the story of Abraham. Knowing God would not kill the righteous along with the wicked, Abraham reminded himself and God that He cannot deny His own nature (Genesis 18:23, 25). He is gracious and longs to deliver the righteous, although He must punish the wicked as well. This understanding propelled Abraham boldly forward in intercession. When we understand God's nature, then we are much more likely to ask Him for help or deliverance.

If we take this same understanding and apply it to our earthly parents, we see more clearly how our relationship with God is foundational to our communication with Him. If our earthly father is always mean and yells at us, and never wants to spend time with us, then we will not want to ask him for help because we would probably just get more yelling. If our earthly father is kind and always trying to help us, then when we have a problem we will go to him and ask for help. Our understanding of God will affect our intercession in the same way. If our understanding of who God is does not align with Scripture or we misunderstand Scripture to paint a picture of God as a wrathful, vengeful God just waiting to punish us for our next wrong action, we will never desire to partner with Him or engage in intercession.

In the story of David having a child with Bathsheba out of wedlock, the child became very sick for a week. During this week, David prayed and fasted because he understood God was full of grace and mercy and David's repentance might release God's mercy for the child to be spared. When the child died, David ate because he knew God's judgment had been released and the matter was settled. But as long as the child was still alive, David sought God's face in persistent intercession because he knew God might choose mercy because he had shown David so much mercy throughout his life. He understood it because he had experienced it. Our experience of God's nature will infuse our intercession with the boldness and persistence needed to see it through to the end.

3. Urgency

As we are wrestling with God in prayer, we are captivated by the urgent nature of God pressing upon us in intercession. We sense the necessity of carrying the burden in such a way as to continually ask, seek and knock until the Lord releases His peace to us. Because of a particular situation, need or sin, we are asking for God's intervening hand. As I quoted in Isaiah earlier about standing in the gap, we must wait patiently while still fervently seeking God's work to come about. Oftentimes, waiting is thought of as a passive exercise, but waiting is an opportunity to fervently seek God's face. As I mentioned, when David's child with Bathsheba was stricken ill by the Lord, David did not just wait to see what God would do. He fervently sought God's face through prayer and fasting to see if God might show mercy. This is the urgency with which we must approach partnership with God. We cannot put off until tomorrow what God has asked of us today. We must strive with God as Jacob did to see the plans and purposes of God released. We must seize the moment God has given us and refuse to let anything stand in the way of seeing God answer our prayer.

In the story about Sodom and Gomorrah, we read of Abraham's continual pleading until he was entreating for only 10 righteous people. His fervency to save Lot and his family as well as for the Lord to have mercy on Sodom and Gomorrah pressed upon his heart until He sensed God's peace wash over him. He had stood in the gap and wrestled with God, though not knowing the result of his prayers. He was confident in God to bring forth His plans and purposes. God sent angels to rescue Lot and his family because there were not 10 righteous people living there, but those who were righteous were rescued. Abraham received his heart's desire for Lot to be saved. While Sodom and Gomorrah were still destroyed, Abraham learned invaluable lessons in partnering with God to bring forth His plans and purposes in the Earth. These lessons are crucial to seeing all of the nations blessed through Abraham.

Contemplation:

Let us not rush by this section without first assessing our own prayer life. Are we stuck in the rut of only considering our own personal needs and wants in our prayer time? Have we set aside time in our daily schedule to listen to the Lord and hear His heart? Are we growing in beholding and enjoying the Lord? Do we revel in His goodness and delight in His mercy?

Next, we must reflect upon our view of God. How do we see God operating in our lives? Is the Lord a taskmaster who asks us to do this and that? Is He a good Father who cares for our every need? If your view of God is not aligning with Scripture, take some time to ask the Lord what has caused this and then ask Him for a Scripture that will combat this lie. God wants our understanding of Him to be that of a Bridegroom who is longing with love to partner with His Bride in the fullness of His Kingdom. Do we see ourselves as the Bride? Are we choosing to co-labor with our lover?

Beyond our own prayer time, are we entering into the place of partnering with God? Have we taken the time to ask the Lord today what is on His heart? The Lord is longing to show us more of His plans and purposes in the Earth. Will we take the time today to enter into the conversation and see how He wants to move?

1. Take some moments to wait on the Lord and ask Him what is on His heart – maybe you will see someone's face or be reminded of a situation; or maybe God will show you a picture of a map and highlight a particular country. Wait on the Lord and ask Him.

2. Take time to ask someone else how you can pray for them today and then actually pray. Maybe there is someone at work who is sick or someone at church who needs God to intervene in their situation. Pray and ask God to move!

Prayer:

Lord Jesus, I surrender my own needs and wants to You. I want to know Your needs and wants today. Grow in me the spirit of prayer to contend for the fullness of Your promises and refuse the enemy's tactics to discourage and dissuade me from seeing God's best in my life. I see now that Your promises are not automatic but require me to pray them into existence. Holy Spirit, give me tenacity and perseverance to be steadfast. Give me the spirit of wisdom and revelation to know what You are saying today, and give me power to instantly obey Your spirit by praying in line with what You say. In the name of Jesus, I pray. AMEN.

8

Fasting

Fasting is an effective method of aligning our hearts with God as we pray. We see the people of God fasting throughout the Old and New Testaments, especially in times when they were in need of greater revelation or desperate circumstances. Whether in the Old or New Testament, fasting is always coupled with prayer. Prayer joined with fasting is a powerful tool in the life of believers.

First, let's look at what is fasting. According to Webster's Dictionary, fasting is to abstain from food and/or drink for a period greater than eight hours. This time of fasting can take many forms. The length of the fast can be from a day to 40 days or more. The type of fast can vary from fasting food and drink for a day to fasting all food for 40 days to only fasting certain food for a period of time. We need to be led by God as to how we should fast because none of these types of fasts earns more points with God than another kind of fast. We do not fast to earn God's favor. We fast because we love Him and want to know more of His ways.

Although in God's Word we will see fasting primarily related to either food or drink or the combination of both, there are other types of fasts today that serve to bring our attention and concentration more deeply upon God. One type of fast is a silence fast. Today, we are constantly bombarded with various forms of communication crying out for our attention. We have mobile phones we can take with us wherever we go, email we can receive on our phone, messages through other forms of media, instant chats, and other apps where we can constantly see what other people are doing.

These communication channels can become a hindrance to hearing God's voice speaking to us. When we have so many people trying to connect with us, we are easily distracted. Today, the need to be connected, to know what is going on, to be up on breaking news can lead to a deafening roar of voices screaming for our attention. Entering into a silence fast where we choose to lay down for a period of time all of the other forms of connecting so we can concentrate on what God is saying is an effective fast in today's culture.

Another type of fast is limiting what you read to only the Bible for a period of time. We choose not to read things on our phone or in other books. Rather, we choose to only feed our spirit with the Word of God for a set time. Similar to fasting food, we are cleansing our minds and thoughts of wrong ways of thinking and limiting ourselves to God's view of circumstances. We choose to set our minds solely upon God's Word and God's ways, and we receive new insight and understanding.

Other types of fasts include fasting a particular meal every day for a period of time. One can also fast particular foods for a period of time. These are all ways for purposefully dying to our flesh in order to deepen our connection with God.

Jesus' Exhortation

In order to better understand the discipline of fasting, let us look at the Sermon on the Mount, where Jesus is speaking to His disciples about how they should live in His Kingdom. First, we see Jesus said "when" the disciples fast. He was not telling them they could do it if they would like. He was not suggesting it as a possible method of earning favor with God. He was saying fasting should be a regular part of their lives. He was assuming the disciples already had this as a routine discipline in their lives. Jesus moved them forward, helping them understand how it should be done and some of the principles of why it should be done.

We do not fast to look more spiritual before other people. We are called to fast in secret because we do it out of love for God and a passion for more of His power and presence to be released in our lives. The Pharisees were very good at fasting. But alas, their concern was not to get closer to God. They were merely doing it as a way to show others their spirituality when in actuality it was all empty rituals. We can do things in the Christian life, but just because they are good things does not mean they are accomplishing anything inside of us. Disciplines are only fruitful in our lives if we are doing them from the right heart motives.

Another false motivation for fasting is to earn God's love or acceptance. Fasting is not about working hard enough or doing a fast for long enough so God will give us certain favor or blessings. Fasting changes our hearts before God and helps us to come into alignment with His plans and purposes in a given situation. By crucifying our flesh, we gain a greater sensitivity to the Spirit and increased understanding of God's desire for us.

Jesus ends with the promise of rewarding those who are faithful to fast in secret, when they do it only unto the Lord and not unto people. This reward is also referred to by Jesus in the previous section of the Sermon on the Mount regarding prayer. Jesus is highlighting the need for true disciples to see the power of doing these disciplines in secret. Prayer as well as prayer joined with fasting are powerful keys in God's Kingdom for unlocking spiritual power and divine revelation if we will do it in God's way. God's promise is to reward those who are faithful. When we are receiving a reward from God's infinite storehouse of resources, we cannot begin to fathom how He will choose to reward His saints. We may need to wait for the reward, but it is doubtless worth the wait.

Principles of Fasting

As we look at the vast number of examples throughout Scripture, we could not possibly cover them all here. Through these examples, we glean principles for effective prayer and fasting in our own lives. These principles will help us to understand the reasons why we pray and fast as well as some guidelines on how to do it effectively.

Beginning in the Old Testament, we see in Judges an early example of fasting as the Israelites inquired of the Lord if they should go to war against their brethren, the tribe of Benjamin. Although the Lord instructed them to go to war, the Israelites lost 22,000 men in battle that day. The next day, they fasted and prayed all day as to whether they should again go against their brethren because they had already sustained significant losses. The people gathered together in unity to pray and fast for God to give them guidance as to how they should proceed. God answered with a clear word to again go to war against the Benjamites. As they fasted and prayed, they received guidance and this produced confidence to obey what they had heard from the Lord (Judges 20). Even though the result was not what they expected, the confidence they received from clearly hearing the Lord through fasting and prayer enabled them to continue the battle rather than give up.

1. Receiving Guidance and Help to Make Decisions

One of the principles of prayer and fasting is that we can receive guidance from the Lord regarding specific requests. Jesus prayed and fasted before selecting the 12 disciples, and the church at Antioch prayed and fasted before sending out Barnabas and Saul. When we want to know the mind of the Lord, fasting helps us to focus on the Lord's thoughts and not our own.[20] We have an increased ability to discern the Lord's will in a particular situation. We will not be swayed by power or position but instead we will only be swayed by the voice of the Lord.

Queen Esther

We see another example of fasting in the story of Esther. Esther became queen of the Persian empire after a lengthy beauty treatment and interview process. The Lord was with her and gave her wisdom about who to trust and what to do in order to gain favor with King Ahasuerus. One of the king's officials, Haman, created a mad scheme to eliminate the Jews in the kingdom by tricking the king into signing a law to be sent throughout the kingdom. When Esther's uncle, Mordecai, learned of the news to annihilate the Jews throughout the land, he sent word to Esther. Esther understood the dilemma, but she also knew if she went to the king without an invitation she could easily be executed. In order to know what to do, she called for a three-day fast for all of the Jews with no food or water. Esther's desperation to know the mind of the Lord caused her to call for a short but radical fast. She did not want to proceed until she knew she had sought the Lord's face for wisdom.

Mordecai exhorted Esther that she had come into this place of position and power for such a time as this. But rather than just following what her mentor said, she fasted and prayed for the Lord's guidance. We should not simply follow the thoughts of people to please them, but we need to be moved by God's voice and His command alone.

Having fasted and prayed, she was confident of God's calling to intercede for her people and stand in the gap. During the fast, she also received wisdom for how to proceed. Without knowing if the king would accept her, she boldly approached the throne. The king extended his royal scepter and beckoned Esther to come, offering her anything up to half the kingdom. Esther approached the king and humbly requested permission to prepare a feast for him along with Haman. Being surprised by this kind invitation, they both gladly accepted. At the banquet, the king again offered Queen Esther anything she desired up to half of the kingdom. But instead, she invited them to another banquet the following day.

Between these two banquets, the Lord made King Ahasuerus restless, and he called for the chronicles to be read. The king realized Mordecai had never been rewarded for saving his life. Contemplating what reward should be given to Mordecai, the king asked Haman how to reward a man the king wants to honor. Haman, thinking only of himself, assumed the king was talking about him and conceived the most lavish display of honor he could imagine; sit the man upon the king's horse, clothe him with a royal robe worn by the king, and then parade him through the streets proclaiming this is the one whom the king desires to honor. Upon learning the man the king wanted to honor was his arch enemy, Mordecai, Haman was crushed. Weeping, he returned home only to have his wife and friends tell him that he would surely fall before Mordecai.

First, the Lord gave Esther the wisdom to throw the king and Haman a banquet which would bring the king's favor and delight as well as throw Haman off his plan. The wisdom Esther had received from the Lord to give not one but two banquets allowed the Lord to speak to the king and create a plan to honor Mordecai before the second banquet even took place. Haman, feeling utterly defeated, was ushered to the banquet with the queen and king. Queen Esther, giving the king two separate banquets, had endeared herself to the king. She sensed the release from the Lord to ask the king for the lives of her and her people. The king's anger was aroused, and he quickly had Haman sent to the gallows for his crime. Furthermore, Esther along with Mordecai wrote letters on behalf of the king to save their people from the horror of annihilation that was coming.

2. Prayer and Fasting Releases Wisdom and Confidence to Act

Prayer and fasting prepared Esther for the difficult circumstances and gave her wisdom to know how to respond in each situation. She was confident in hearing God's voice and obeying what He asked her to do. Fasting joined with prayer releases guidance in how to proceed in difficult circumstances. Fasting also produces confidence to know what God is calling us to do. This confidence releases energy to obey no matter what the consequences may be. Fasting also allowed Esther to hear God's timeline and not rush to asking the king the first day. God's timing is always perfect, and waiting on Him releases greater results.

Jonah

Another example of fasting is found in the book of Jonah. There are actually two separate incidences of fasting in the book of Jonah. First, we read of Jonah running away from God's calling to go and proclaim repentance among the people of Nineveh. Nineveh was the capital city of the Assyrian empire, the arch-enemy of Israel at this time. Jonah did not want to go and proclaim repentance to the people of Nineveh because he knew that if they repented then God would forgive them and not destroy them. Jonah wanted to see the destruction of his enemies, but God desired to have mercy if they would only repent.

This amazing story of God's desire to have mercy on people outside of the Israelites was a foreshadowing of the gospel going to the Gentiles after the coming of Christ. God's heart has always been for all peoples to worship Him, for the whole Earth to be filled with His praises. Jonah wished God would start with some other people group that was not his arch enemy. This story reminds us of Jesus' words in the Sermon on the Mount; we are blessed when we love our enemies because anyone can love someone who loves them, but we must be filled with God Himself to love our enemies. God was demonstrating His unfathomable love to not just love our friends but even our enemies.

However, Jonah's heart was not right. He was not ready to love his enemies, and he did not want God to save them. He wanted to see them utterly destroyed by God's wrath. So Jonah ran in the opposite direction of Nineveh, hoping to escape God's call. But the Lord found Jonah on a ship and sent a great storm so that the people were forced to throw Jonah overboard to save their lives and the ship. The Lord then sent a large fish to swallow Jonah. He was in the fish neither eating nor drinking for three days in a forced fast, much like Esther's fast for the lives of her people. He finally came to the end of himself and realized God was with him no matter where he went. God is not only in Israel. God is with us wherever we go. He surrendered and committed himself to do what he had promised and to fulfill the call of God to go to Nineveh.

3. Prayer and Fasting Purifies Our Hearts

The fasting and prayer of Jonah purified his soul of all of the secret arguments that he had for not obeying. The fasting and prayer allowed him to see the situation from God's perspective instead of his own small point of view. His eyes were opened to see that he could not run from God. God is not only in one place, which was the common view back then. He understood in a new way God's sovereignty, whether in one country and people or another, whether on land or in the depths of the sea. We could almost hear Jonah recalling David's psalm,

> "Where can I go from Your Spirit? Or where can I flee from your presence? If I ascend into heaven, You are there; If I make my bed in hell, behold, You are there. If I take the wings of the morning, and dwell in the uttermost parts of the sea, even there Your hand shall lead me, and Your right hand shall hold me" (Psalm 139:7-10).

Jonah came face to face with the greatness of God, His infinite goodness to find us and call us back to Himself. His inability to escape God's presence confronted him with the dilemma of how to move forward. He repented and realigned himself with God, *"But I will sacrifice to You with the voice of thanksgiving; I will pay what I have vowed"* (Jonah 2:9). In the painful resignation, he offered up the sacrifice of praise and thanksgiving for saving his life and chose to give God his obedience.

Second, we see the people of Nineveh responded to Jonah's cry for repentance from God's coming judgment and destruction of Nineveh. The people of Nineveh took heed to the warning and proclaimed a fast, followed by a royal declaration from the king for all of the people to fast and pray and turn from their wickedness. This stunning turn of events showed the power of the Almighty God to turn hearts that are ready to hear his message. This people had heard of the power of the God of Abraham, Isaac and Israel. They had seen Israel's enemies defeated by this powerful God. Now, this great God beckoned to them to turn from their evil ways before He destroyed them completely.

God's heart is not just moved by people fasting, but this is an outward sign of an inner reality of seeing their great need for God and desperation for His salvation. This story of God's mercy testifies of His desire to pour out His mercy on anyone who would come to Him in true repentance, turn from their wickedness, and desire to follow after His ways.

4. Prayer and Fasting Produces Humility and Love

Fasting produces humility and love for God in our hearts. As we deny our natural desires, we realize how frail we really are and how much we are dependent upon God. Jonah came face to face with his dependence upon God; David, by fasting for his child with Bathsheba embraced this humility, convinced of his dependence upon God; Ezra needed to know what to do and he deliberately humbled himself through fasting to know the mind of the Lord (Ezra 8:21).

Through this humility, we begin to see our sin in the light of God's holiness. The least bit of sin and pride will block our prayers from being answered. God's holiness shows us our sin and enlightens us to see the sin that is blocking our prayers. In light of His holiness, we are empowered to align with God's heart and follow His ways. Fasting deepens our humility and enables our prayers to be more effective (1 Peter 5:6, 2 Chronicles 7:14, James 4:10, 1 Peter 5:5). [21]

This humility increases our ability to respond to God. This humility also increases our love for God. In Psalm 116, we read, *"I love the Lord because He has heard my voice and my supplication."* Our love is a direct result of the overflow of God's interaction with us. The more we see God's love for us through His response to our prayer and fasting, the more we will love God in response to this experience.

Jesus' Temptation in the Wilderness

Here, we encounter one of the most well-known passages of Scripture regarding fasting. Before Jesus entered into public ministry, He took time to fast and pray for 40 days and nights. Jesus knew He would experience much opposition along the way as well as encounter passionate crowds who would come to Him for teaching and healing. The importance of beginning well in ministry cannot be overstated. By taking time to fast and pray, Jesus was prioritizing doing ministry according to the Father's plan. He did not want to do things His own way, but He only wanted to do what He saw the Father already doing.

During His time in the wilderness, Jesus encountered the enemy trying to make Him stumble at His weakest moment. Jesus embraced humility while His flesh was weak, and instead He relied on the Spirit to help Him. Satan's repeated temptations failed, but through Jesus' reliance upon the Holy Spirit He was enabled to overcome. We cannot overcome the enemy in our flesh. Only through dependence upon the Spirit and God's Word can we also be victorious.

5. Fasting Increases Revelation and Understanding of the Word of God

Jesus overcame these temptations by responding with the Word of God. He did not rely on the wisdom of man but on the wisdom of God. God's Word has power to break every chain and set us free from every temptation. Satan repeatedly tried to tempt Jesus, even trying to trap Jesus by quoting the Word of God but misapplying it. By fasting, Jesus' heart was prepared with an increased revelation into the Word of God. Daniel experienced the same revelation through his fasting. He wanted to understand the vision he had, so he fasted for 21 days. Through fasting, Daniel received the revelation and understanding he was seeking regarding the vision recorded earlier in Scripture (Daniel 9-10).

6. Regular Times of Prayer and Fasting

Jesus' example of fasting and praying did not end with His experience in the wilderness. Jesus continued in the discipline of praying and fasting throughout His ministry. He consistently chose to go up on the mountain by Himself to pray. These regular times of prayer and fasting enabled Him to consistently follow the Father in ministry. Continuing to remind Himself of His need for the Spirit's help, He set an example for us as we continue in ministry. We also must find regular times to get away and fast and pray for God's leading and guidance. This habitual leaning on the Lord in humility enables us to realign ourselves before the Lord.

This discipline of Jesus to regularly fast and pray has been repeated throughout the centuries of church history with profound results. We see in the lives of John Wesley, Charles Finney, David Brainerd and many others the discipline to fast one or two days every week. These regular times of prayer and fasting served to remind them of their dependence upon God and call them to a deeper place of humility before God. Fasting enabled them to be more conscious of the sin in their lives and released power to overcome it. The times spent crying out for God to move were all the more powerful because they were careful to walk before the Lord in holiness and righteousness. God is able to use those who are consciously depending on Him as their source.

7. Steps for Fasting

Fasting is not difficult, but it is uncomfortable to the flesh. It is not a natural idea to not eat when every fiber of our being is crying out for food. Fasting requires us to lay hold of our supernatural nature. We have to purpose in our flesh to say that we want more of God than we do food, Facebook, TV, our phones, or anything else we might be fasting from. This discipline gives a practical dimension to the more spiritual dimension of brokenness.

Brokenness calls us to deny ourselves and take up our cross. Fasting is a practical way to deny ourselves in the flesh and commit ourselves once again to following hard after God. In those moments of temptation to take a bite of something or check Facebook, ask the Holy Spirit for the power to say no and walk away. These seemingly small temptations give us small glimpses into how we need to do this in our spiritual lives as well. When we run into temptation, we need to ask for more of the Spirit to fill us and help us to flee the temptation. The Spirit wants to help us, but we must ask for help. So many heavenly resources are available to us, but we do not lay hold of them and use them in our spiritual lives. Imagine being a construction worker with a tool belt wrapped around our waist, but we never use any of the tools. We cannot expect to grow in our faith if we are not using the tools and resources available to us. Fasting in the natural releases feasting in the spiritual realm where our spiritual lives can grow in greater dimensions.[22]

For some people, fasting may be a relatively new discipline they have not personally practiced or heard much about. If fasting is new to you, start with one day. Here are some practical steps for engaging in fasting.

First, create a clear prayer list for the fast.

Second, ask the Lord for a specific time frame for the fast. For example, one day or three days or some other time frame. Then ask the Lord what type of fast – a water-only fast, water and juice, only vegetables, only one meal a day, silence fast, or something else. For longer fasts, it is often helpful to prepare physically before the fast by not having coffee for a few days before beginning. For those who have not fasted before, it would be wise to consult with a doctor regarding any health concerns.

Third, fast with someone else. Find a friend willing to fast on the same days. They may want to fast in a different way, but the important part is to fast and pray about the same prayer topics (Acts 13:2; 14:23).

Fourth, prepare for spiritual warfare because fasting is most disturbing to the enemy. Fasting is one of the weapons we use during spiritual warfare, which we will discuss more in the next chapter.

During the fast:

Begin by humbling yourself before the Lord. Ask the Holy Spirit to come and search your heart for any sin and repent of anything the Lord brings to mind.

Take time to read the Word of God in an increased fashion. Ask the Lord for spiritual insight and revelation in His Word. Sometimes, it is helpful to study a particular book of the Bible or passage of Scripture during the fast.

Fast in secret. Don't schedule a lunch with a friend and then not eat. Be purposeful to engage in prayer during meal times.

If you fail, don't give in to condemnation. Get back up the next day and go for it again.

After the fast has finished, break the fast gradually if it is an extended fast of more than a few days. Start with simple foods before eating a big meal.

Application:

Fasting is an important discipline for every disciple to practice. Whether young or old, it is always a good time to start fasting. Perhaps we have done it once, but it is not a regular part of our walk with the Lord. Set a goal to fast once a quarter or once a month. Ask the Lord to highlight someone with whom you could fast. If married, do it together as a couple. This important spiritual discipline will open up new areas of growth and deepen your relationship with the Lord.

1. What is your goal for growing in this discipline of fasting? Who will you ask to hold you accountable and maybe even fast with you as you grow in this?

2. Who is one person you could encourage with what you have learned about fasting? We all have the same access to the Lord spiritually, but whether or not we use the tools available to us is up to us. Encourage

someone else to press into the fullness of all of the resources available through Christ.

Prayer:

Lord Jesus, I ask You to deepen my hunger to know You more. Increase my desire to fast and pray as a regular part of my walk with You. I want to grow in the spirit of revelation regarding the Word of God. Open my eyes to see new things and to hear Your voice more clearly. In Jesus' name I pray, AMEN.

9

Spiritual Warfare

One of the important topics for growing in a lifestyle of abandoned devotion is encountering spiritual warfare. In our journey, we can often become distracted and dry, lazy and complacent, defeated and hopeless. But the Lord has called us to live the victorious Christian life. So, how can one reconcile these feelings with the truth of Scripture? We are called to wage war until we see the victorious life available in Scripture evident in our lives. We cannot settle for what our feelings tell us is true. We cannot be okay with average or dry. We are called to seek first the Kingdom of God and His righteousness and then the Lord will take care of the rest (Matthew 6:33). It is easy to be on fire for God for a month or a year, but we are called to walk in this intimate, wholehearted devotion for the rest of our lives. The key to unlocking this consistency lies in the vigilance to continue in spiritual warfare.

Committing ourselves to spiritual warfare requires perseverance. It is not an easy road as we war against the enemy of our souls. The enemy would love nothing more than to see us fail and not get up again. But God's endless mercy beckons us to get up and run back to Him once again. Even when we have wandered far from God's love, He calls to us to return to Him again, return to our first love. Returning to the

Lord requires repenting for the sin that has taken us away from Him. Returning challenges us to deepen our humility and see our desperate need for Him, as did the prodigal son as he returned to the Father. When we persevere in returning to Him, we taste the sweetness of that intimate relationship once again, the tenderness of the Father's embrace, the blessedness of restoration into His presence filled with peace and joy.

The Lord is committed to producing the fruit of His Spirit inside of us. Through spiritual warfare, we contend for the fullness of God to dwell in us, but the adversary does not want us to experience the fullness of God inside us because there would be a greater dimension of the Kingdom released into the world. As God's righteousness is displayed in our lives, God's power is also released in a greater measure. God's power operating in our lives brings forth victory in the circumstances around us.

As God manifests the fruit of His Spirit in us, He also wants to give us the spirit of wisdom and revelation in the knowledge of Him. God wants to take us deeper in understanding His ways and His character, but the enemy wants to keep us in the dark. The enemy specializes in lies and twisted truths, which produce more bondage and a lack of intimacy in our relationship with God. For example, if we are believing the Lord is a God of wrath, vengeful and angry with us, then we will be slow to repent because we are afraid of God's wrath being poured out on us. If we feel God is always angry, then we will rarely pray because why would God help me if He is angry with me? These lies shape our behavior and responses to God in ways we do not even realize. As God releases wisdom and revelation, we see the fullness of God's destiny for us and how He wants to set us free from our old nature so we can enter into His plans. We want to embrace the fullness of who God is as a loving Father, a faithful friend, and a just and wise King. The more we see these to be true, the more it will change our response. We will respond in love to those who offend us because, though we offended God, we were still loved completely by Him.

Our Reality Today

It is easy to fall into some extreme tendencies when we are talking about spiritual warfare. One extreme is to want to ignore Satan. This camp would say that Satan is real, but we are not going to focus on him. We want more of God so we should just focus on developing intimacy with Him. While this is good and right – that our relationship with God does take focus and determination – we cannot pretend that Satan does not exist by ignoring him or what he does. Paul the apostle challenges us to not be ignorant of Satan and his ways. Satan loves to sow unforgiveness and bitterness. He loves to break relationships by creating doubt, division and discord. We must be careful not to let the enemy creep in unnoticed.

The Call to Watch and Pray

Part of our call to enter into spiritual warfare begins by being watchful. Throughout the gospels, we hear Jesus calling us to watch. We see it in the parable of the 10 virgins, this call to take heed to our walk with God so we do not become like the foolish who had no oil. We see it again in the Garden of Gethsemane. Jesus beckoned to Peter, James and John to watch with Him in prayer. In Matthew 26:41, Jesus, implored them saying, *"Could you not watch with Me one hour? Watch and pray, lest you enter into temptation. The spirit indeed is willing, but the flesh is weak."* Jesus is highlighting one of the keys in spiritual warfare. We can avoid so much trouble if we will be vigilant over our walk with God and watchful over our relationships. Too quickly we let our flesh make decisions because it is the easy way out or it feels comfortable. But the Lord is calling us to challenge the flesh and say "yes" to the Spirit inside of us. However, we will not be able to say "yes" to the Spirit if we are not being watchful in prayer, sensitive to the Spirit's leading.

While we could discuss many important issues at play in spiritual warfare, there are four unique principles about which we must have a deeper understanding in order to achieve victory in this critical realm of abandoned devotion:

1. Authority

One tendency is to attribute to Satan too much power and authority. Satan is not like God. Just because Satan is unseen, he does not have the same power and authority.

Only God is sovereign, and He has all authority over all things. Authority refers to jurisdiction and governmental influence or position. Rulers over a particular area have authority to make decisions and laws and to exercise power. Satan has the authority or the ability to exercise power on the Earth because of Adam and Eve's sin in the Garden. At the Fall, the authority and dominion they had been given by God was relinquished to Satan. However, when Jesus went to the cross and paid the price with His sinless life and then rose from the grave, He defeated the power of the enemy and restored the authority, dominion and victory for all believers. This same authority has been given to us as sons and daughters of God. God wants us to live lives where we are experiencing His victorious Kingdom. He wants us to use His authority to enforce the victory and push back the kingdom of darkness. Christ's authority available to all believers is greater than the power of Satan, but it requires believers to enforce that victory in our everyday situations.

However, Satan's authority is limited. Satan does not have authority over believers unless granted to him by God. Two instructive examples in Scripture of God allowing Satan to sift a believer in order to encourage spiritual growth involve Job and Peter.

In the life of Job, the Lord was watching over His people, and He saw Job who walked before Him, blamelessly – fearing God and shunning evil. Satan talked with God and said that of course Job followed God because he was blessed on every side, but if the blessings were taken away then he would not follow after God in the same way. This testing was allowed by God to reveal the depths of Job's heart and whether he would turn away from God when circumstances became difficult. Job passed the test and did not blame God for the difficulties. Seeing the greatness of God, he humbled himself and surrendered to the wisdom of God.

Likewise, in the Gospel of Luke we see Peter was sifted. Satan knew God had great things ahead for Peter. Satan thought if he could only get Peter off course early then he might be able to derail his destiny. Jesus said to Peter, *"Simon, Simon! Indeed, Satan has asked for you, that he may sift you as wheat, but I have prayed for you, that your faith should not fail; and when you have returned to Me, strengthen your brethren"* (Luke 22:31-32). Jesus was praying for Peter! He knew the trials that Peter would face, and yet Jesus did not make the trials disappear. Trials are not something to be avoided. James wrote, "Count it all joy when you fall into various trials, knowing that the testing of your faith produces patience" (James 1:2-3). James highlighted the key of our faith development, responding to trials correctly. James expected joy to erupt in our hearts when we face trials because the trials are God's gift to us to make us more like His Son, Jesus.

These verses give us insight into the trials and temptations that we go through in life. The enemy is trying to move us off course. He is hoping we fail the test and turn away from following the Lord. But Jesus is also praying for us, and He desires for us to grow in faith through the trials and then use these experiences to encourage and strengthen others who are facing the same trials. The testings we face refine our faith. We must choose to draw closer through the difficult circumstances and not allow our hearts to grow hard or our faith to become cold.

2. Power

God is omnipotent, all powerful. God's power is unlimited. We cannot even fathom the rich resources at His disposal. God's power is not limited by even the nature of His own creation. In nature, wet wood does not burn. But when Elijah prayed after pouring water over the wood and the altar, God sent fire that consumed the sacrifice, the wood, the stones and the dust, and that licked up the water in the trench around the altar (1 Kings 18:33-38). As a sign to Hezekiah that the Lord would heal him and deliver him from the hand of the king of Assyria, the Lord made the sun go backward 10 degrees (Isaiah 38:8). We know today that the sun does not move, but the Earth is rotating on its axis. The Earth would have to reverse the direction of its rotation in order for the sun to appear to go backward 10 degrees. This is not a normal occurrence in God's creation.

As a sign to Moses in the wilderness to get his attention, the Lord sent an angel into the midst of a burning bush, a bush burning with fire that was not consumed (Exodus 3:2). It is the nature of fire, as we saw in the story of Elijah, to consume everything. Yet, the Lord made the bush burn without destroying it. Luke records the story of the disciples sailing to the other side of the sea with Jesus asleep in the boat. As a great windstorm arose, the disciples panicked because the boat was beginning to fill with water. Desperate, they woke Jesus up. He merely spoke to the wind and waves, and the storm ceased. The disciples marveled that even creation obeyed His commands.

God's power is not limited to what we can imagine or even what we think are the limits of His own creation. All creation is from God and moves according to His command. We are only limited by our expectation of God. It can be easy to fall into the trap of thinking healing can only come through medicine or deliverance only through people because these things are tangible things we can see. But God is the God of the miraculous. We should not limit the God of the universe to our limited understanding.

3. Knowledge

Only God is omniscient, all knowing. God knows the number of hairs on our heads, and He also knows our thoughts, everything we do, and our words before we even say them (Psalm 139:1-6). We cannot comprehend the depths of God's knowledge about us and the world around us. There is nothing about us that God does not know. He knows why we do certain things a particular way. He understands our heart even when we do not understand it ourselves.

Satan's knowledge is limited. False prophets have knowledge, but it is incomplete. They do not know the end from the beginning. They cannot show how one thing will affect another. Satan looks at patterns, and out of those patterns he has created fortune tellers, astrologers, psychics and the occult. These mediums appear to have knowledge, but it is based solely in what can be seen.

In 1 Kings 22, we see an interesting picture of knowledge from two different perspectives. Ahab, the king of Israel, and Jehoshaphat, the king of Judah, planned to fight Ramoth-gilead. Before going out to fight, they consulted the prophets of Israel. About 400 prophets gathered together, and the kings asked them if they should indeed fight against Ramoth-gilead. All of the prophets agreed that the kings should go into battle for they were sure to win. But King Jehoshaphat was unsure about these prophets and asked if there was a prophet of the Lord. His request for a 'prophet of the Lord' implied a person who had a track record of hearing from the Lord.

Indeed, there was one, Micaiah, but King Ahab did not like him because he usually did not prophecy good things for Ahab. Nevertheless, Micaiah was summoned, and he inquired of the Lord. He came back with the same response the other prophets had said – that they should go to war for they would surely be victorious. However, Ahab was wary because this was the first time Micaiah had ever prophesied good for him. When Ahab pressed Micaiah to see if he was telling the truth, Micaiah said that he had actually seen all of Israel scattered like sheep without a shepherd.

Ahab had expected this evil report, but Micaiah explained. This explanation showed the limitation of knowledge by those who were not close to the Lord. The Lord had determined it was time for Ahab to die, so he allowed a lying demonic spirit to speak to the prophets in order to persuade Ahab to go out to battle. This lying spirit was only too happy to oblige and help send someone to their death. When the prophet of the Lord inquired, he actually understood the whole picture with complete knowledge of what was happening, because the Lord did nothing without first showing His prophets. However, because it was the Lord's will for Ahab to die in battle, the prophet of the Lord gave the same message as the false prophets the first time. Zedekiah, one of the other prophets, was offended at Micaiah for saying he listened to a lying spirit. Those who do not walk closely with the Lord can easily be deceived by the enemy with false knowledge. Only those walking according to the Lord's ways and in step with His Spirit will be entrusted with the knowledge of His plans and purposes in the Earth.

4. Presence

Only God is omnipresent, present everywhere simultaneously. God can talk to the more than seven billion people on the planet all at the same time. He can be with every believer all the time without being less present to someone else. The story of Jonah is a wonderful example of God's presence with us no matter where we go (Jonah 1-4). The Lord told Jonah to go to Nineveh, but Jonah went in the other direction. He got on a boat to get away from his calling, and the Lord created a storm on the sea. Jonah tried to avoid the storm, and God, by jumping into the ocean. But in the water, a fish swallowed Jonah. Jonah, no longer able to escape, understood God's presence was inescapable and chose to submit to God's calling to go to Nineveh.

Satan is limited in where he can be at one time. He cannot be everywhere at once. He can send demons to different places, but he himself cannot be in more than one place at one time. We see this in the case of the man possessed by many demons from Gadarenes. The demons ask Jesus to cast them into the swine. They could not be in the man and swine at the same time. The demons go from one place to another.

In the book of Job, we see clearly Satan's limitation of being only in one place at one time. The Lord had been looking over the angels and the hosts of heaven, and Satan came to the gathering. God asked Satan what he had been doing. Satan replied he had been walking back and forth over the face of the Earth. Satan could not see everything at once. He had to walk around the Earth to see what was going on with people and know whom he should harass. Satan had to go case by case and assess what trouble he could create on the Earth.

Principles for Victory in Spiritual Warfare

Spiritual warfare is a part of the life of a disciple. Throughout the Old and New Testaments, we see the struggle of believers portrayed in many different ways. In the Old Testament, often other peoples came against the Israelites in battle. This warfare in the natural was symbolic of the warfare in the spiritual realm. Kings and rulers of other nations also oppressed the Israelites. Under this oppression, the Israelites had to learn how to live victoriously. The same was true of the church in the New Testament. Facing oppression from the Roman government and others throughout history, the church needed to stand firm without compromise. From these examples, we can grow in understanding how to overcome spiritual warfare.

1. Victory comes to those who are surrendered to God.

Victory in spiritual warfare begins in the place of surrender and humility before the Lord. When we enter into the battle with our spirit surrendered and desperate for God's intervention in our midst, we position ourselves for victory. In Exodus 17, Moses interceded on the mountain while Joshua fought the battle. As long as Moses had his hands raised in surrender, Joshua experienced the victory. But the moment Moses put his hands down, Joshua began losing ground. The posture of Moses with his hands raised is a picture of surrender. Moses saw the evidence in Joshua's battle of the importance of his surrender. There is a clear connection to the victory we experience directly related to the level of surrender in our hearts. Victory comes as we are relying upon God. If we are depending upon ourselves to fix the problem or find a solution, then we will quickly find ourselves in a chaotic mess. Trials are meant to be an avenue through which we draw closer to God, not for turning our back on Him by trying to solve them by ourselves. If we are patient in our surrender, the Lord will bring about the victory.

Spiritual authority comes from a life wholeheartedly devoted to God. We must live out our surrender not only in a desperate plea, but also by wholly giving ourselves over to the Lord. If we are lacking in obedience, then we will lack in spiritual authority as well. Spiritual authority is necessary if we want to war victoriously. Wesley Duewel writes, "A half-and-half Christian is of little use to God or man. He or she cannot prevail when necessary and cannot use the name of Jesus with any sense of spiritual authority. Total commitment, total obedience, and a life filled and refilled with the Holy Spirit are the only basis for empowered, authoritative use of the name of Jesus. To pray in the name of Jesus is to pray out of a life that is Christlike" *(Mighty Prevailing Prayer,* p. 280). When we are living a life completely surrendered, we can exercise the spiritual authority necessary to see power released and the victory complete.

2. Fasting enables us to understand God's strategies for overcoming our trials.

Through fasting, our hearts are tenderized to receive from the Lord the strategy and wisdom He wants to give us in order to see the victory attained in our circumstances. Fasting is also another way of surrendering to God. The act of fasting demonstrates our utter dependence and desperate need for God to show us the way forward. We often face a problem and immediately begin to fix it without waiting on the Lord for His plan. In 1 Chronicles 20, King Jehoshaphat was faced with an enormous army coming against him. Although he was afraid, he chose to seek the Lord and call a fast for all of Judah. We cannot let our emotions determine our actions but instead act by faith and trust the Lord for His plan.

The Lord is looking for people who are willing to seek His face in prayer to see His plans and purposes accomplished in the Earth. Arthur Matthews writes, "In any situation where Satan dominates and threatens, God looks for a man through whom He may declare war on the enemy. He purposes that through that man Satan be served notice to back up, pack up, and clear out" (Mathews, Born for Battle, p. 62). When we sense the enemy dominating or threatening, we need to tune into the Spirit because God has a plan for victory if we are ready to receive it. God's model for His Kingdom is partnership with His people to see His plans accomplished. It is the same in spiritual warfare as it is in discipleship. We are called to partner with God to advance His Kingdom in the Earth.

Another powerful example of fasting is in the book of Daniel. Daniel had received a vision and message, but he did not understand what it was about. So, he set himself to fast and pray for three full weeks in order to gain understanding and revelation concerning the vision he received. His fast was to abstain from meat, wine or other desirable food – sweet things or delicacies. As Daniel was an official in the government, he ate with the royal household and would have daily been served a feast of food including wine, meat, and many other pleasing dishes.

The most striking part is Daniel's glimpse into the supernatural realm. From the first moment Daniel set his heart to pray, the angel was released to come to him. But then he encountered resistance and warfare. Sometimes in our situations, there will be a delay before the victory comes. We must hold on with perseverance to see the victory come to pass. If Daniel had given up before he got to the 21st day, he would not have received the revelation. Wesley Duewel wrote, "When you long to strengthen and discipline your prayer habits and to add a new dimension to your prevailing in prayer, add fasting. When you seek to humble yourself before God in total submission to His will and in total dependence on His almighty power, add fasting. When you face an overwhelming need, a human impossibility, and your soul hungers to see God intervene by supernatural power, add fasting" (*Duewel, Mighty Prevailing Prayer,* p. 183). The Lord hears our prayers, and He is answering our cries. Though the answer is delayed, do not give up! The answer is on the way!

3. A key strategy for victory in spiritual warfare is worship.

Worship causes us to fix our eyes upon God rather than on our circumstances. By rightly adjusting our gaze, we are able to get a fresh perspective on the trial we are facing. The prophet Jahaziel spoke to King Jehoshaphat about the strategy necessary for winning the battle against the Ammonites. He said, *"Position yourselves, stand still and see the salvation of the Lord"* (2 Chronicles 20:17). The people positioned themselves in worship, declaring God's praise and worshipping His character as a God of holiness and mercy; and as they did this, God set ambushes against the Ammonites. Worship is powerful. Enemies are destroyed as we worship the Lord. Sometimes, when we do not know what to do, the best thing is to begin to worship the Lord, lifting up our voices in praise and adoration of who He is.

This is one of reasons the book of Psalms is so powerful as a prayer guide. We can read and pray the Psalms as one of the tools through which we can overcome the enemy. In the Psalms, we see countless examples of David facing desperate circumstances, but he ends in the place of praise and adoration. For example, in Psalm 61, David begins by saying that his heart is overwhelmed. By the end of the psalm, David writes, *"So I will sing praise to Your name forever, that I may daily perform my vows."* Having poured out his frustration in prayer, he realigns himself with God's presence through worship, focusing on God's greatness and majesty.

4. Victory comes as we rest in God's strength and not in our own.

In the account of the prophet Jahaziel, we read his call for them to "stand still." Gaining the victory in spiritual warfare is not accomplished through our own striving through the flesh. We are called to rest and rely on God alone to obtain the victory. This same theme is seen with Moses in Exodus 17. He was supposed to keep his hands raised, but as his hands got weary he chose to sit down. He did not try to lean on the power of his flesh to keep his hands raised, but rather he chose to rest in the place of surrender, believing God would obtain the victory. Resting means trusting and not doubting that God will intervene. Resting is the peaceful spirit of victory. We do not need to be anxious but through prayer commit our situation to God and rest with peace, knowing He will take care of it.

Paul writes, *"Finally, my brethren, be strong in the Lord, and in the power of His might"* (Ephesians 6:10). Our strength rests in God's might. We are equipped to stand as we rely on His power and not on our own. Often, we have to come to the end of ourselves and realize our own weakness before we can embrace His strength. We are called to be strong in the Lord, understand our identity in Him and acknowledge the power of His work in our lives. Paul also reminds us in 2 Corinthians 12 that it is in our weakness Christ's strength is made perfect. We need to embrace our weakness so the fullness of Christ's strength can dwell within us.

5. We are most effective in spiritual warfare when we do not do it alone.

As we are going through trials and struggles, the Lord has created the body of Christ to come alongside one another. Depending on the circumstances, we can come alongside in different ways. In some cases, we need someone who can keep us accountable in a particular area. Maybe we need someone to fast and pray with us, like Esther asked her maids to fast with her before she went into the king. Fasting and praying in unity is fruitful, especially when we are seeking guidance in a particular situation. At other times, we need people who will help us when we are weary, which we see when Aaron and Hur held up Moses' hands. And sometimes, we need people who will join in the battle and fight with us through prayer and worship. Joshua did not fight the battle alone. He had an army united with him to fight alongside him. The anointing and power released as we join in unity with others will help break the power of the enemy. Relying on other people to join with us makes us vulnerable and fosters humility in which the Spirit can freely move.

6. Praying the Word of God releases power.

In Ephesians 6, Paul reminds us our struggle is not with flesh and blood, but rather with principalities and powers. Therefore, we must employ spiritual weapons to fight spiritual battles. We must strengthen ourselves, being girded with truth – the Word of God – receiving it as our daily manna. We must feast upon it to nourish our spirits. Not only is the Word of God, the belt of truth, a defensive part of our armor, but it is also the sword of the Spirit. The sword is an offensive weapon. When the Lord highlights a particular Scripture as we are praying or reading, that Scripture becomes an offensive weapon to attack the enemy and bring about the victory. Andrew Murray wrote, "Little of the Word with little prayer is death to the spiritual life. Much of the Word with little prayer gives a sickly life. Much prayer with little of the Word gives more life, but without steadfastness. A full measure of the Word and prayer each day gives a healthy and powerful life" (*Murray, Prayer Life*, p. 88).

But a sword does nothing if it lies on the ground. No matter how sharp the sword is, it cannot accomplish anything lying there. We must be listening to the Spirit so we can hear what He is saying and then use it in prayer. As we pray the Scriptures, we are wielding the sword against the enemy, cutting down every scheme and plan to steal, kill and destroy the saints.

7. Warfare begins in our thoughts.

We can end the battle before it begins if we will follow Paul's admonition to *"take every thought captive to obedience to Christ"* (2 Corinthians 10:5). This is an essential step most believers overlook. We can easily let our thoughts run astray without being watchful about the content of our thoughts. We dismiss any notion of it not being of God because it is just in our head, we did not actually do something.

However, in Jesus' Sermon on the Mount, this is the very thing He emphasizes. He is not just concerned with murder but with the depth of anger in our hearts. He not only wants us to put away adultery, but to take heed to ourselves regarding lust. It is these heart-level issues swirling around in our thoughts that we need to take captive and remind ourselves they do not align with Jesus' heart.

We remember well King David, who started out by being lazy, and decided not to go to war with his men. But walking about on his roof, he saw Bathsheba bathing and then inquired after her. Knowing she was married, David sent a messenger to bring her to him. David's laziness turned to lust, and, instead of taking that thought captive right there, he committed adultery followed by murder. We have a choice about how we will respond to every thought. Will we take it captive and see if it aligns with Scripture or continue unhindered with our own plans?

8. We wage warfare from the position of victory.

Jesus has already defeated the enemy. The glorious reality of our faith is that we can read in Revelation how the story will end. Christ has purchased the ultimate victory for us to reign with Him through His blood. Paul writes, *"Having disarmed principalities and power, He made a public spectacle of them, triumphing over them in it"* (Colossians 2:15). This victory through the cross will be brought to completion in the age to come when He returns to establish His Kingdom on the Earth and eventually to rid the Earth of evil once and for all. As disciples who are walking according to His ways, we have been given the power to advance His Kingdom through the proclamation of His gospel. We are on the winning side of the epic battle. We are able to win every battle through God's power if we do it God's way and are faithful to live wholeheartedly for Him alone.

The Reality of Spiritual Warfare

Spiritual warfare is a constant reality for every believer. Even Jesus faced spiritual warfare as He was establishing His Kingdom here on Earth. After being baptized by John in the Jordan River, Jesus in humility is led by the Spirit into the wilderness for 40 days and nights to fast and pray as the strategy for overcoming the enemy. Then, at the end of the

40 days when Jesus is at his weakest point physically, the enemy comes to tempt Him. Physically exhausted, Satan begins by tempting Him with food. But while Jesus' flesh is weak, His Spirit is strong from the fasting. Clearly seeing Satan's tactics, Jesus counters with the truth in the Word of God. Satan repeatedly attempts to trick Jesus, but He is not fooled because the fasting has increased His discernment. Fasting strengthened His perseverance in the face of the temptation and His resolve to defeat the enemy.

Not only did Jesus face temptation in the wilderness, but He was constantly surrounded by Pharisees who wanted to catch Jesus contradicting the law of Moses. He had multiple encounters with people who were possessed by demons. Not only did He face trials with those who were on the periphery of His ministry, He also faced the ultimate betrayal of one of His own 12 disciples, who handed Him over to the Pharisees to be hung on a cross. By a kiss, Jesus understood the depths of spiritual warfare both from without and from within. Yet, He remained the spotless Lamb, with no sin or blemish of even the smallest measure.

Paul the apostle also faced such strong spiritual warfare that he directly wrote in his letters twice on how to combat it. He also makes mention of Satan or trials that he faced such as beatings, imprisonment, tumults, evil reports, and many other various trials. James, the leader of the church in Jerusalem, counseled his people to count it all joy when faced with various trials because it is through this spiritual warfare that faith is refined and purified. Peter calls us to the same suffering that Christ endured; ready to be reviled for doing good and following the example of Christ.

Application:

Spiritual warfare is real. Looking back over the last year of our lives, do we see the different trials we have gone through as spiritual battles? It is often easy to rationalize conflict and problems in our lives as mere natural circumstances. But we need to revisit Paul's words that we are not wrestling against flesh and blood, but against principalities and powers. Recognizing spiritual warfare is only half of the battle.

Satan would love nothing more than to lure us off course so we don't fulfill the destiny God has for us. We need to be watchful over our lives, careful to take heed of our personal walk with the Lord as well as of our ministry to others.

Have we seen God's victory in the spiritual battles we have faced? Are we battling from God's position of victory or do we start the battle feeling defeated? Are we letting the spiritual warfare distract us from following after God's calling?

1. What is one principle the Lord is highlighting for you to implement in your life related to spiritual warfare? How can you strengthen your understanding and application in your personal walk with the Lord? Some ideas might include praying more of the Word of God as a way to stand against the lies of the enemy, spending more time in worship when you feel overwhelmed, practicing taking thoughts captive as soon as they enter your mind and choosing not to dwell on things that don't align with the Word.

2. Do you know someone who has been experiencing a tough situation? What is one principle the Lord has taught you that you can share? Our experience with God is our testimony. This is one of the most powerful weapons we possess, for with it we are able to overcome the enemy (Revelation 12:11).

Prayer:

Lord Jesus, I want to grow in watchfulness in my life, being vigilant to guard my time in the Word of God and prayer as sacred and holy. Open my eyes to see You at work in my daily life. Give me the spiritual discernment to see where the enemy is at work around me. Create in me a deeper hunger to live according to Your ways and walk in step with

Your Spirit so that I am always ready and equipped with the spiritual authority necessary in every situation. Holy Spirit, make me sensitive to Your leading in how to walk out Your plan of victory in my life. In Jesus' name I pray, AMEN.

10

Committing to a Lifestyle

The movements of the heart and the habits of abandoned devotion are keys that can bring new spiritual depth to a believer. The level of our spiritual depth is determined by how consistently we pursue this abandoned devotion as a lifestyle. Anyone can jump on the latest thing and do it for a month or even a year, but true growth and maturity happens when we are committed to it as a lifestyle for as long as we live. Of course, we will have times when we fail, but we do not let our failures determine our destiny. We repent and run back to the Father, who is waiting with open arms to receive us. We want to continually move into new realms of faith and trust in God. We do not want to get stuck in the realm of faith God gave us a year ago. Rather, we want God to stretch us beyond our comfort zone so we are completely dependent upon Him.

The term "radical" is often used in Christian circles to describe someone who is going hard after God. However, mostly these radical believers catch fire for a month or a year and then fizzle out. Truly radical believers are those who have been walking the abandoned devotion lifestyle for 20, 30, 40 years and are still going strong. This does not mean those people have not faced trials or hardships. It means they have not let the trials destroy their faith. They have not let ministry crowd out their personal time with the Lord.

In order to be people who are continually growing in their faith, we want to look at five keys that will enable us to be people who have followed the Lord consistently over a lifetime. These keys will guide us in those times when our spiritual life seems to be dry or we do not see the fulfillment of the promises God has given to us over the years. We will look at the need for a growing commitment to the Great Commission, consistency, ever-increasing faith, praying in the promises, patience with God's timing, and movement toward maturity.

Growing Commitment to the Great Commission

Those who are pursuing the abandoned devotion lifestyle will be marked by a growing commitment to the Great Commission. The Great Commission is not just the concern of a few believers, rather it is the concern of every true disciple. God's heartbeat for all nations to worship before His throne is not something that was tacked on at the end of the gospel, but it is the over arching theme of redemption for all humanity connecting the whole Bible. Committed followers will be growing in their understanding of the Great Commission and discipling others in this core identity of the Church. True disciples are those cultivating their role in the Great Commission, not just looking for message bearers to complete the Great Commission. The whole Church is called to be involved in the Great Commission, and every disciple needs to engage in the Great Commission whether through prayer, sending, going, mobilizing, advocating or welcoming. As we are becoming more like Jesus, the natural overflow of our lives will mirror the love of God for every tribe, language, people, and nation.

The Need for Consistency

The first key to walking out the *abandoned devotion lifestyle* is consistency. Today, people are caught up in the next new trend. Even in a news feed, we find the stories that are trending right now. The danger of following the latest trend is that we can lose sight of the disciplines that keep us grounded in our faith. We can get busy trying this new thing or that new thing rather than being diligent to stick with the core realities that have been the building blocks of our faith. Trends come and go, but being steadfast is where we will see fruitfulness.

Our consistency needs to be rooted in faithfulness in the small things. "Small things" do not mean unimportant things. Small things refer to the habits we have discussed in the earlier chapters of reading and studying the Word of God, praying, fasting, and engaging in spiritual warfare. We will go through seasons when we may not hear the voice of God speaking as regularly. We will go through seasons when reading the Word of God will seem more like a chore rather than a joy. We will go through times when we do not feel as close to God in intimacy as we have in other times. We may do a fast during one of our regular times and not sense that anything has changed, no great revelation, no answer to prayer, no understanding from the Word of God.

There is a temptation when we do not feel like God is speaking to stop resisting spiritual warfare. We give in to the temptation to stop fasting because we begin to think it really is not that effective anyway. Eventually, we do not read the Word of God. This is a dangerous road. The moment we stop engaging in the habits, we will begin to lose the avenues through which God can speak to us again. Without reading the Word of God, we will eventually stop engaging in the other habits of an effective life in God.

But the good news is, if we stick with the habits of reading God's Word, praying, fasting, and engaging in spiritual warfare, then that season will not last forever. If we consistently set aside the same time every day to read the Word of God and pray, we will once again hear God's voice speaking to us. If we choose to fast even when it does not seem to be changing us, we will see a difference over time. We must choose to worship God even when we do not feel like doing it. The Lord at times draws back to test our heart and our commitment to Him. We cannot waiver in our devotion. We must continue to press upward in the high calling God has for us.

When we are faithful in the small things, the ebbs and flows of life do not seem as high or low because our heart is not moved by those outward things. Our heart is kept constant by the intimate relationship we have with the Lord. If we lose our job, we will not be depressed because our hope was not in our job but in the Lord. If we get promoted at work, we do not suddenly think more of ourselves than we should because our core identity is found in being a son or daughter of the King of kings.

We do not need to have a big ministry or to be able to say we have led such and such number of people to the Lord. Our calling is to be faithful with what the Lord has put in our hands. If we have people around us, we should be discipling them. If we are gifted to work with children, then we should be training them up in the ways of the Lord. We are not called to be jealous or envious about the size or fame of another's ministry. The calling is to faithfully multiply whatever small things He has entrusted to us.

Ever-increasing Faith

Second, God wants us to have ever-increasing faith in every area of our lives. We are supposed to be moving into greater amounts of dependence on the Lord. If we are trusting God for the same thing last year as we are expecting this year, then we really have not grown in faith. When we have already seen God move in one way, then it is easier to believe God the next time for the same thing because He has already done it. The challenge is to continue to increase the faith dimension of our walk with God.

Some examples of ever-increasing faith can look very different. An evangelist believed the Lord to bring 10 people to her who were ready to receive the gospel. Ask God to increase the amount to 15 or 20. A friend goes to church and feels a burden to pray over people, and she was able to pray for five people after the services. Ask the Lord to send people who need prayer at the grocery store, in the mall, at work. A student of mine had to trust the Lord for $800 for her airfare to come to Thailand. She reserved the ticket and then prayed faithfully. The night before she had to get on the plane, she had an unexpected knock on her front door. A friend from church had come with the exact amount of money that she needed to get on the flight. In the future, God will ask her to trust Him for more than $800 because she has already seen God move at that level before. These experiences of ever-increasing faith do not necessarily grow day by day but season by season. As we are being led by the Spirit in prayer, we step out in faith. We do not want fear to determine our destiny in God. If God has put a dream in our heart, we must continue to pray and believe until we see it come to pass.

Our ever-increasing faith must be based upon God's Word, and trust must increase from listening to the still small voice. As we are studying God's Word and walking obediently in a lifestyle of prayer, the Lord will challenge us to go beyond trusting in the things that we know according to our minds. Instead, we will need to trust in the things that we have not seen in order to see the breakthrough the Lord wants to bring in our lives.

In Luke 5, Peter had been fishing all night and caught nothing. As a wise fisherman of many years, he knew intellectually the best time to go fishing was at night. Not only going at night, but Peter also knew the best spots where the fish tended to gather. He came back from fishing discouraged and a bit depressed. But he heard a man preaching like he had never heard before. The words were coming with such authority and power he listened eagerly to soak up every word.

Jesus came to speak with him and told him to go fishing in the middle of the day. Although Jesus' words were contrary to everything Peter had learned about fishing, he recognized an authority in Jesus' words that captured his heart and caused him to respond with, "Nevertheless, at Your word." Peter could have raised many objections to Jesus' command, but rather than argue he responded in humility and obedience with faith. We, like Peter, can cultivate this response of faith by being faithful to study God's Word and to listen for Him to speak to us. Ever-increasing faith is Christ's goal for us; choosing to believe that nothing is impossible, no matter how much we are stretched beyond what we have known before.

Praying in the Promises

God calls us to partner with Him in this life of faith through praying in the promises He has given to us. In our time of studying God's word and praying, we will hear God speaking certain promises to us. These promises can come through the Word of God, through a friend giving us a prophetic word, through a dream or vision, as we are reading a book, or in other ways. It is easy to think that the promise we have received is going to happen tomorrow. However, it is rare for a word to come to pass quickly. Instead, as we read through the Bible, we see God delaying the fulfillment of the promises in order to generate dependence on Him to fulfill those promises. God desires us to develop relationship. If the Lord fulfilled the word as soon as we received it, then we would see God as a type of Santa Claus whose main job is to give us good gifts. Rather, the delay of God's promises calls us into a deeper lifestyle of prayer as we wait to see these things come to pass. We develop the muscles of dependence, knowing we cannot bring about the promises ourselves but that we are truly dependent upon God to bring forth His promise in His timing.

We see throughout Scripture promises are often delayed because God knows we need time to ready to receive the promise. The time of waiting and praying is a time of preparation so when the fulfillment comes we are ready with the spiritual fortitude and humility necessary to receive the promise. If the promise comes too quickly, pride rises up and we lose the very thing that had been promised.

Patience With God's Timing

As we seek God in prayer for His promises to be released, we are also growing in patience. We see many examples throughout Scripture where people received a promise and then had to wait 10 to 40 years to see those promises come to pass. Abraham waited 25 years from when he was promised a son until Isaac was born. Joseph had the dreams of his family bowing down to him when he was approximately 16 years old, and he went through 14 years of rejection, slavery, hardship and imprisonment before he saw the fulfillment of his dream at the age of 30. David was anointed king by Samuel at the age of about 16; but he had to suffer through being hunted by Saul and being constantly on the run for 14 years before he saw the partial fulfillment of God's promise at the age of 30, becoming king over Judah, and then had to wait seven and a half more years before he was crowned king over all 12 tribes.

When Caleb was 40 years old, Moses sent him as a spy into the Promised Land to survey the land and to see what kind of people lived there. Although 10 of the spies brought back an evil report, Caleb responded with faith, saying the land was good and they could take it because the Lord is with them. His response of faith is rewarded by the Lord with a special inheritance in the Promised Land for Caleb and his descendants. However, Caleb waited 45 years to see this promise fulfilled. His waiting was not just sitting back and waiting for God to move, but he and his tribe participated in conquering the Promised Land to see all 12 tribes attain the land.

Waiting for the promises of God is not just about praying them in but also cooperating with the Lord and remaining faithful in the small things so that when the promises are fulfilled we are not overcome with pride but instead with gratefulness and praise for the work the Lord has done. Guarding our hearts with humility and continually surrendering His promises back to Him for His glory to be revealed in His timing will bring Him the most glory. If we begin trying to bring forth God's promises in our flesh or in our own timing, we are no longer in the will of God. We might use the excuse that the Lord has promised us something, but God is not fooled. He knows we are working outside of what He has designed for us. We see this with Abraham and Sarah. They were promised a child, and when God delayed to bring forth the promise, they decided to take things into their own hands and have a child through Hagar. Not only did this bring division, jealousy, even hatred within Abraham's family, but the lasting result was a son of Abraham which was not part of God's plan; so Ishmael had to be sent away.

Movement Toward Maturity

Through all of the movements of the *abandoned devotion lifestyle* and engaging in the habits that keep us connected to the Vine, the Father is moving us upward toward the goal of being fully like His Son. He will be continually watching over us, hedging us into His path of righteousness, putting thorns in those places where we wander off the path to cause us to return to Him again and again, and preparing us for His glorious return. The path we are on in the Christian life is one that continually becomes both steeper and more narrow. The longer we have walked with the Lord, the more He expects from us. The greater our revelation about God's ways and His character, the greater the amount of accountability and standard of righteousness He expects.

The Father is not content to leave us where we are. He has great plans for our future, which are primarily rooted in the depth of our experience of His presence and in greater knowledge of His ways. He is burdened for those who do not long for His presence; He is challenging those who have become comfortable church sitters instead of Presence seekers, willing to sit rather than engage; He is pursuing those who have His Word burning inside of them, for to those who have, more will be given.

Our maturity is the Father's primary goal. He is not as concerned about the numbers of people with whom we have shared the gospel or the number of places we have traveled. He is intensely concerned with the depth of relationship we have with Him. Have we grown in knowing Him more than we did last year? Do we understand things about the Father's character and Kingdom we had not known before? Are we growing in our hatred of sin? Are we growing in our sensitivity to hearing God's voice? Are we moving toward more quickly obeying the

Spirit when we are prompted to do something? Are we being faithful to share what we are learning with those around us? Are we influencing those around us to grow toward maturity as well?

Application:

Looking back over the course of your life with God, take some time to analyze these five areas: consistency, ever-increasing faith, praying in the promises, patience with God's timing, and moving toward maturity.

1. What is the strongest area in your life with God? Ask God to continue to grow these foundations and your love for Him through this area. Where do you feel weakest? Ask God to show you how to grow in this area and put it into practice this week.

2. What is one area that you could share with a friend? God calls us "great" when we not only obey Him ourselves but teach others to do the same (Matthew 5:19). "Teaching" does not mean you are out in front of others. Sharing with someone from your own experience is often the most powerful teaching to impact someone's life.

Prayer:

Lord, I want to continually grow in loving You with all my heart, soul, mind and strength. I ask, Holy Spirit, for You to come and search me and show me those areas where You want to stretch me. Open up to me new revelation because, as I see You more clearly, I will love You more. I want to be ever-growing as Your disciple and finish well in this life as a faithful witness of Your love and grace so I may hear those precious words, "Enter into the joy of your Lord!" I pray this in Jesus' name. AMEN.

Bibliography

Bickle, Mike. *After God's Own Heart*. Lake Mary, FL: Charisma House, 2009.

Bickle, Mike. *Growing in Prayer: A Real-life Guide to Talking with God*. Lake Mary, FL: Charisma House, 2014.

Bounds, E.M. *On Prayer*. New Kensington, PA: Whitaker House, 1997.

Clinton, James Robert. *The Making of a Leader: Recognizing the Lessons and Stages of Leadership Development*. Colorado Springs, CO: NavPress, 1988.

Duewel, Wesley. *Mighty Prevailing Prayer*. Grand Rapids, MI: Zondervan, 1990.

Duewel, Wesley. *Revival Fire*. Grand Rapids: Zondervan Publishing House, 1995.

Hession, Roy. *The Calvary Road*. Fort Washington, Pennsylvania: Christian Literature Crusade Publications, 2002. p. 21-34.

Lawrence, Brother. *The Practice of the Presence of God*. New Kensington, PA: Whitaker House, 1982.

Lightfoot, John. "Introduction to Matthew". *"John Lightfoot's Commentary on the Gospels"*. https://truthaccordingtoscripture.com/commentaries/jlc/matthew.php#.YnTG59ozZPY.

Metaxas, Eric. *Bonhoeffer: Pastor, Martyr, Prophet, Spy*. Nashville: Thomas Nelson, 2010.

Murray, Andrew. *Humility: The Beauty of Holiness*. Fort Washington, PA: Christian Literature Crusade, 1995.

Murray, Andrew. *Key to the Missionary Problem*. Fort Washington, PA: Christian Literature Crusade Publications, 1988.

Murray, Andrew. *With Christ in the School of Prayer*. New Kensington, PA: Whitaker House, 1981.

Pink, A.W. *Profiting from the Word*. Carlisle, PA: The Banner of Truth Trust, 1985.

Sheets, Dutch. *Intercessory Prayer*. Ventura, CA: Regal, 1996.

Endnotes

[1] James Robert Clinton, The Making of a Leader. Colorado Springs, CO: NavPress, 1988, p.155.

[2] Andrew Murray, Key to the Missionary Problem. Fort Washington, PA: Christian Literature Crusade Publications, 1988, p. 74.

[3] Eric Metaxas, Bonhoeffer: Pastor, Martyr, Prophet, Spy. Nashville: Thomas Nelson, 2010. p. 384.

[4] Mike Bickle, After God's Own Heart. Lake Mary, FL: Charisma House, 2009. p. 111.

[5] Brother Lawrence, The Practice of the Presence of God. New Kensington, PA: Whitaker House, 1982, p.33.

[6] Andrew Murray, Abide in Christ. Fort Washington, PA: Christian Literature Crusade Publications, 1997, p. 24.

[7] Trotter, Baker's Dictionary, "Grace," https://www.biblestudytools.com/dictionaries/bakers-evangelical-dictionary/grace.html

[8] A.W. Pink, Profiting from the Word. Carlisle, PA: The Banner of Truth Trust, 1985, p. 11.

[9] Jack W. Hayford, Prayer is Invading the Impossible. South Plainfield, NJ: Logos International, 1977, p. 92.

[10] John Wesley, A Plain Account of Christian Perfection, The Works of John Wesley (1872 ed. by Thomas Jackson), vol. 11, # 29, pp. 366-446

[11] Bounds, E.M. On Prayer. New Kensington, PA: Whitaker House, 1997, p. 11.

[12] Wesley Duewel, Revival Fire, Grand Rapids: Zondervan Publishing House, 1995, p. 53.

[13] Ibid, p. 102.

[14] Dutch Sheets, Intercessory Prayer, Ventura, CA: Regal, 1996, p. 29.

[15] Murray, Humility, p. 14.

[16] Bounds, On Prayer, p. 294, 296.

[17] Bounds, On Prayer, p. 290.

[18] McIntyre, Hidden Life of Prayer, p. 87.

[19] Murray, With Christ in the School of Prayer, p. 70.

[20] Bickle, After God's Own Heart, p. 134.

[21] Duewel, Mighty Prevailing Prayer, p. 188.

[22] Bickle, After God's Own Heart, p. 139.

GLOBAL
MISSION
MOBILIZATION
INITIATIVE

GlobalMMI.net

GMMI serves the global Church as a resourcing ministry for the growing mission mobilization movement through:

- Mobilizing tools, strategies, prayer initiatives, conferences

- Equipping trainings, internships, teachings, materials

Core Objectives:

- Multiplying mission mobilization movements (within national associations, church/ denomination/ organization networks, local ministries) using proven strategies

- Empowering mission mobilizers who mobilize, coach, and equip ministry structures

- Producing high quality, strategic, mobilizing, and equipping tools, materials and resources serving the global Church

- Discerning and emphasizing biblical, Spirit-led models and core messages of mission mobilization through teaching resources, training schools and courses

- Cultivating a spiritual community in Chiang Mai, Thailand, of interns, staff and students strengthening the mission mobilization movement globally

- Spiritually contending (through prayer, worship, as a voice, training, perseverance) for all God wants to release through mission mobilization in the global Church

OTHER RESOURCES FROM IGNITE MEDIA

Cultivating Abandoned Devotion to Jesus

God is calling His people into deeper relationship with Himself. This is the beginning of all effective ministry and the only way effective ministry is continuously sustained. We cultivate this wholeheartedness through studying His word deeply while applying all we are learning. These bible studies go deep into the heart of God's Word, revealing depths and insights that will revolutionize your spiritual life. These can be used individually or in a group setting.

- Studies in the Life of Joseph
- Studies in the Book of Jonah
- Studies in the Book of Colossians
- Studies in the Sermon on the Mount
- Studies in the Parables of the Kingdom (Matthew)
- Studies in the Seven Churches of Revelation
- Studies in Matthew 24-25 Jesus' End Times Discourse

Mobilizing Local Ministries

The Holy Spirit is raising a vision of not merely one by one mission mobilization, but the concept of mobilizing and equipping whole local ministries for Jesus' Great Commission.

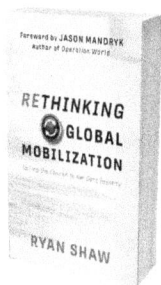

- Rethinking Global Mobilization
- Handbook for Great Commission Ministries (English, Spanish, French, Chinese - Simplified and Traditional, Thai)
- Great Commission Bible Studies
- Global Prayer Teams
- Six Roles for Every Believer in the Great Commission
- Developing a Sending Strategy
- Waking the Giant

Equipping for Global Harvest

To see the literal fulfillment of the Great Commission we need to be equipped in certain areas often not discussed or emphasized. These resources provide focus on core areas of equipping the Holy Spirit is highlighting and that need to be carefully grasped and integrated into our lives if we want to be effective.

- Engaging the Holy Spirit
- Declare His Glory Among the Nations
- Proclaiming the Kingdom
- Spiritual Equipping for Mission
- Abandoned to Jesus

www.ingramcontent.com/pod-product-compliance
Lightning Source LLC
Chambersburg PA
CBHW060749050426
42449CB00008B/1326